1 MONTH OF
FREE
READING

at

www.ForgottenBooks.com

By purchasing this book you are eligible for one month membership to ForgottenBooks.com, giving you unlimited access to our entire collection of over 1,000,000 titles via our web site and mobile apps.

To claim your free month visit:

www.forgottenbooks.com/free788864

ISBN 978-0-483-56768-9
PIBN 10788864

PREFACE.

Works on art must not only explain but justify themselves; if their vitality is not sufficient to do this, all the recommendations in the world cannot save them from an early death.

The author of the explanatory text of this work, acting in conjunction with Arthur von Ramberg, in fathering those children of the Muse which are here offered to the public, prefers therefore to send this book into the world without any sponsor, and to let it make its own way. The result has justified his decision, for the voices of the police authorities of criticism, who have examined into the legitimacy of these brain-children, as they have appeared one by one, or serially, so to speak, have agreed in this at least, that they have sound bodily health, if not fine manners; and the public, whose business it is to support them, has received them with surprising readiness.

It is just this that lays upon us the duty of uttering a few words of apology for such of our little flock as are not well washed and kempt. Against coolness one can arm himself with pride, but kindness at once opens the heart to gratitude and a sense of unworthiness. Both of the fathers knew well that the reception given to their progeny has been, and must be, all the more friendly in proportion to the closeness with which these brain-children repeat in themselves the features of their mother, the Muse of SCHILLER.

Who could fail to love her? Whose heart has she not made to glow with her look, when he on whom her eyes have fallen was young and full of noble aspirations? Whom has she not had the power to elevate, move, warm, and fill with renewed youth, on meeting her in the autumn of life, and looking again upon the beautiful and gentle Muse who once stirred the youthful feelings with such powerful promptings? If we once looked upon her with adoration, only to lose her from sight in the later storms of life, even if not to disown her, our astonishment will be all the greater to find, on meeting her again, that Schiller's Muse is to be prized all the higher, the more she is understood. What she was before to our heart, she becomes subsequently to our mind; we see a new side of our goddess, and she, who once took our senses captive by her fascinating charms, now elevates us even while she sets us free from her slighter and more ephemeral allurements.

Children, confessedly, resemble not the mother alone,

but the father as well. If this is an inevitable evil, it is no less so in our case, where the peculiarities of the fathers' are much more obvious than those of the mother. But if in any one of these art-children there is any thing that may remind the observer of the graceful Schiller Muse, its fortune is secure. To attain the whole vast perfection, the lofty elevation of that Muse, cannot be dreamed of. There is not a painter in Germany who is competent to portray adequately Schiller's characters, and still less can the German engravers pretend to such a measure of skill. Still, if the artist must abandon all hope of attaining the whole beauty and loftiness of the original, and of grasping all the thought which animates and glorifies each feature, he can at least try to observe closely, and reproduce faithfully. He will not fail in this case to create a living work, and one whose similarity to the original will be all the more marked, the more salient he tries to make its individuality. The fancy of the observer, thoroughly acquainted with the original, will be stimulated to fill out that which the artist was not able to reach. This is the fundamental thought which has guided the efforts of both of us in the drawings which are now laid before the reader.

If even the photographs of well-known persons seem to one to be faithful portraits, while they are unrecognizable by another, it is unquestionable that in the free creation of forms, whose individuality is the dictation of the imagination alone, there must be scope for the gravest varieties of opinion. And this will be more certainly the case when, as here, the original drawing cannot be published, only an engraved copy of it, where, however marked the success, there will be something of the excellence of the drawing wanting, and where, be the success indifferent, the best half never reaches the public eye.

The difficulty of engraving has offered the more obstacles, inasmuch as the undertaking now presented to the public is the first one of the kind. Illustrations heretofore have been done either on wood or in lightly-engraved outlines, this style answering better the efforts of the idealizing German school to give a general characterization than to individualize closely. A course so entirely opposed to the one hitherto followed must meet many hinderances. Draftsmen and engravers have gallantly sought to overcome these obstacles, and many plates of our collection give honorable testimony that, in the case of the engravers, these efforts have not been in vain. We, at least, cherish the belief that our work need not fear comparison with similar undertakings out of Germany, and for the very reason that we have not copied foreign productions. The connoisseur will readily confess that, much as he may criticise rightfully in us, not only our faults but our merits are our own.

Enjoying the favorable support of the public, we shall hope to make profitable use of the experience which we gain in this work in the Goethe Gallery, which is in contemplation; and shall enter upon the preparation of it with new courage and hope.

Schiller's life itself exhibits such a continuous and unwearied struggle after perfection, as to form an illustrious example for every German. We hope that it may be said of us that, in our attempts, we have sought to render it due honor.

A few words may be permitted respecting the explanatory remarks which the author has added to the engravings, and for which he alone is responsible. He is the less able to assert that he has added any thing new respecting the poet, that he must frankly confess his ignorance of what is old and already written. It has always been his preference to enjoy the poet himself, instead of studying critics and commentators; and where he has found the need of assistance, he has confined himself to the admirable hints which Gervinus and Julian Schmidt have thrown out. It is not necessary here to repeat in full what he himself has reached unaided, or what he has received from others, since the drawing and the text will be found mutually explanatory and illustrative.

Before this work was commenced, the author, in

common, probably, with most of his countrymen, suffered
from the misfortune of not having read, but having
merely devoured, Schiller, in his youth — of having
learned his melodious verses by heart, but with very
slight appreciation of their value. He had been en-
tranced by only one side of Schiller's genius—the pomp
and glory of his language, and the glowing colors with
which he has painted an ideal world, and set it over
against the world of reality. The man who has no mind
in himself, has little appreciation of mind in another.
And the author, like so many in the period of youth,
contented himself with merely recalling certain sonorous
sentences ; and, at last, on entering manhood, and ex-
periencing the reaction of that period, those sentences,
once so lofty and grand, appeared of doubtful value, and
made him look contemptuously on the poet for years.

The problem that we all have to solve is this : to take
the ideals of youth with us into our maturer years,
reanimate them, give the beautiful form and the lofty
word definiteness and meaning ; to unite the ideal and
the actual world, so as to make the former of service to
the latter, instead of carrying them both around in our
consciousness alienated, the one despised and denied by
the other, because we know not how to construct a
bridge to bind them together.

It needs a long and rich experience of life to make

one capable of this; to so far endow a man that he shall
not deny the possibility of the ideal, and close his eyes
upon it, instead of seeking and finding a divine element
in what is human. And yet, in this very way, every
sound nature is to come back to those ideals of youth,
which ordinarily rest upon a solid foundation.

The author had, for a considerable while, devoted
himself to these studies, when the publishers of this
work communicated to him their intention of undertaking the Schiller Gallery, and requested him to assume
the task. The original plan was that the work should
form a kind of pendant to the English works—the
Women of the Bible and the Characters of Shakespeare,
the German editions of which have been published by
the same house whence the Schiller Gallery issues. The
centennial celebration of Schiller's birth has seemed the
most appropriate time to honor his memory by a work,
the scope of which has hitherto had no parallel. We
have heretofore had representations of Schiller's heroes
and heroines, but no such collective illustrations of his
works as would answer the demands of the present day.

The resemblance between this volume and the two
which have just been alluded to, is only external. The
work is neither French nor English, but German. It
must be a far closer study of the poet's meaning than
any foreign work which exists, if we would truly, and

with pious deference, interpret all his wealth of meaning. The author would scarcely have ventured to undertake a work of so much difficulty, had he not had the good fortune to secure the artistic cooperation of his richly-endowed friend Arthur von Ramberg.

In commencing his task, and more especially in preparing the illustrative remarks, the author entered upon a renewed and thorough study of the poet; and must confess again, as at the outset of this preface, that in these later readings the genius of Schiller has appeared grander, richer, and more powerful than ever in his youth; and that these later impressions prove themselves abiding. The public now receives the result of these studies, and it is to be presupposed that it will be most acceptable to those who come by a similar experience into relations with Schiller. If the work is less acceptable to others, they need enjoy none the less with his immortal muse; for it is the truest indication of classic works of art that they give to every one a feeling of lofty satisfaction; that they offer something to every one, and vary their gift according to the character and training of each recipient.

Munich, *October*, 1859.

F. Pecht.

LIST OF ENGRAVINGS.

FREDERICK SCHILLER.

———

IT is not the object of the following lines to give a biographical sketch of our most universally-beloved poet, but only to throw out a few hints in grasping his personality, as it is expressed in our likeness of him. The portrait which we give, varies from those which are usually met, and leads us necessarily to the manner in which his genius is displayed in his face. This method is peculiar, not only to the likeness of the poet, but will form the basis of our method of treating most of the characters found in his works. Our space will limit us to few and brief remarks.

Great and generous natures are often accustomed to nurture within themselves characteristics which are, apparently, directly antagonistic. This they do for the very reason that they are able to unite these opposite phases, and to reach results far beyond those granted to more simple souls. This is, in an eminent degree, the case with Schiller; and the will-power is the very kernel of his nature.

It is the general custom of writers to regard Schiller as the representative of idealism in our poetry and Goethe as that of realism. It is not to be denied that the former displays everywhere a marked tendency to idealize, and that this spreads splendor and nobleness over every thing that he executes; but to us his real artistic talent appears to lie much more on the realistic side. With every artist it is important to discriminate between that which he desires to do and that which he really does. With the lower orders of minds the thing reached is of a much more ordinary character than the thing purposed; with Schiller, on the contrary, the thing done is often better than the thing aimed at. As abstract ideals, his characters are often without marked personality as originally conceived; but, in the elaboration, they come out quite different, and gain an individuality of life, which gives them much more value than what the poet originally designed. Our inventive faculty is in a measure subject to our control, a fact hinted at even by language itself, one of the truest guides in psychology, to find out being directly connected with to find (in German, *finden* and *erfinden*). In many of Schiller's characters there is, consequently, a certain contradiction between their speech and their action; the poet now following his inspiration, which never misled him, and now his preconceived idea, which often, as in the " Bride of Messina," led him in entirely false directions. That, in the main, he followed the inspiration of composition, is one of the best proofs of his high poetic faculty; all the more conclusive that, in his greatest passages, he always does so. Schiller's often-quoted lines express his own view :

> " What in song shall live,
> Must not in life survive." *

One might conclude from this—and the romantic school has even done so—that the essence of poetry is past, dead, in what has become history or myth. On the contrary, it consists rather in what has life, as Schiller's own works show, which everywhere are best when they lock themselves closest to the interests of his time, whether it be in Wallenstein painting the apotheosis of German chivalry, portraying in the hero a character such as Napoleon's rising star presented to his own gaze ; or in Tell, representing the struggle of a noble German tribe against a foreign yoke—a thought altogether too familiar to Schiller at that time ; or in the "Robbers," and "Love and Intrigue," inveighing against the social conditions of his day and land ; or in Don Carlos pleading the claims of cultivated men on the state ; everywhere his poetry contradicts and overthrows his own theory. His characters are taken from real life, and those which approximate closest to reality are always better than his ideals—the latter, Marquis Posa Verrina, Louisa Millar, Thekla, etc., cannot be compared in poetic merit with his portraits, such as Wallenstein, Tell, Octavio Piccolomini, and others. His ability in

> * " Was im Gedicht soll leben,
> Muss im Leben untergehen ! "

picturing real life is all the more remarkable that, in ·
the multiplicity of details which he constantly gives us,
we scarcely find a hint that, like Goethe, he busied
himself with observing real life. On the contrary, he
overlooked it, left it behind, isolated himself from it as
much as possible. And just as a genuine painter is
constantly giving attention to the form and color of
objects around him without knowing it or wishing it,
so Schiller was constantly studying objects, and treas-
uring them in his memory, without really wishing to
do so.

This unconscious gathering up of treasures, which
his fantasy was subsequently to use, is the true mother
of that artistic intuition so eminently displayed in
Schiller. Above every thing else, the artist has therefore sought to exhibit in his portrait the poet as we
find him in Schiller. As the tendency to idealize is so
prominent a feature of his muse, as there is in him something unquestionably abstract, something alien to the
world of experience, the poet is represented in an
attitude rather looking inward, rather listening to the
voice of his own inspirations than contemplating objects around him. He has something of a seer's and
prophet's air, he is occupied solely with what is great
and exalted; and, as Goethe says, so finely and fittingly
of his deceased friend, one must seek

"Behind him, in the empty space,
What binds us all, the commonplace."

Conjoined with this prophetic gift, there is that super-human power of his that seizes us, and bears us away on the soaring pinions of his glowing enthusiasm, to a loftier height than any other German poet has been able to reach. His broad, firmly-collected brow is the seal of his strength and loftiness, his earnestness and depth; the glance of his eye shows the dreamy reverie, and his other features, rugged and alien, worthily complete his face, and out of their antagonism chime in a lofty harmony.

Schiller was, above all things, a poet, but he was also, and we may say it with emphasis, a Suabian. And, with all its skill and rich endowments, with all its manly strength and decisiveness, this branch of the great German family is probably the least approachable of all—the most crabbed, hardest, least docile, most stubborn, least pliable, and most passionate. These qualities were doubtless observable in our Schiller; the cross-grained, proud, and retiring nature, the impatience, the fierce glow of hate as well as of love, all worked powerfully in this timid, reserved, and intractable spirit. The Suabian peculiarities manifest themselves very clearly in the defiantly raised under-lip, the broad fixed chin, the strong cheek-bones, the markedly defined features. You may see also the nervousness of the thinker who wrought late into the night; and who was so accustomed to regard his body as the mere slave of his spirit, that he was snatched so prematurely away.

This makes it clear that the personality of that Schiller of whom we have so many traces—red-haired, pale, tall, and emaciated—is a mixture of timidity, fear, and even antipathy, which, nevertheless, found such a mighty counterpoise in the massiveness of his genius as to transform dislike into reverence and enthusiasm, even when intimacy with him was forbidden. It is a matter always to be joyed over, therefore, that while in Goethe we have the most harmonious of characters, a personality the most brilliantly furnished both within and without, that any modern nation has displayed in its poets, we have in Schiller the most illustrious example of a spirit, whose own lofty nobility is able to glorify all that was ignoble in the form that contained it.

Fr. Pecht del.   A. Fleischmann sew

CHARLOTTE VON LENGEFELD.

As "a blooming child," with the Graces and Joy as her companions, Lotte encountered the young poet, ...

... ... later ... ... just like a ... girl, ... communicative in society, and was all the more silent in ... ... circle of her home. A cheerfulness, humbleness, and natural good-humor appear in every line of the first year's correspondence, which Schiller's daughter, Baroness Gleichen-Russwurm, has lately presented to us; but, at the very outset, it is nothing but her youthful freshness and gracefulness which interest us in her.

Soon after that fleeting visit to Rudolstadt, Schiller met her again in Weimar, where he ... ... decidedly drawn to her. The correspondence, now in our possession, arose from an interchange of books. ...

CHARLOTTE VON LENGEFELD.

As "a blooming child, with the Graces and Joy as her companions," Lottie encountered the young poet, when, in the society of his friend Wolzogen, subsequently the husband of the older sister, Caroline, he first visited Rudolstadt and the Lengefeld mansion. At a later period, she herself says that, just like a young girl, little communicative in society, she was all the more silent in the intimate circle of her home. A cheerfulness, nimbleness, and natural good-humor appear in every line of the first year's correspondence which Schiller's daughter, Baroness Gleichen-Russwurm, has lately presented to us ; but, at the very outset, it is nothing but her youthful freshness and gracefulness which interest us in her.

Soon after that fleeting visit to Rudolstadt, Schiller met her again in Weimar, where he felt himself decidedly drawn to her. The correspondence, now in our possession, arose from an interchange of books. After the return of the two sisters to Rudolstadt, the correspondence was continued, and led, the next summer, to

Schiller's passing several months in the neighborhood of Rudolstadt, where they accustomed themselves to walks and mutual visits—he to give of his intellectual resources, she to receive. This went on so happily, and with such zeal, that, in the successive letters, one can almost see how the spirited, bright, and yet entirely unlearned girl, was intellectually growing. It was in this period of pleasant summer-walks, amid the cheerful Thuringian hills, when the lovers met almost every day on the meadows or in the wood, that the artist has represented Lottie, in the fair period of first love, when the young man, now looking dreamily within himself, now rapt with enthusiasm, with the flash of genius upon his pale brow, poured out his spiritual wealth, and took captive the heart and senses of the girl just ripening into womanhood. Externally, the affair seemed to be exactly the reverse : the young, lively, and spirited girl, made more easy and familiar with the ways of the world through her intercourse with the court and the noble families of the neighborhood, than was the timid, sensitive poet, would seem to have attracted him, and bound him all the more closely to herself, inasmuch as their relations at that time had merely the form of simple friendship; and neither Schiller nor Charlotte appears to have recognized a warmer feeling. It would seem that the older sister, Caroline, the more gifted of the two, would more naturally have charmed him, since, in her strong tendency to cultivate herself, and her ripe under-

standing, he found what more closely bound him to herself; but, as we never seek what we ourselves have, the
freshness which he found in the younger gained the
victory in his heart over the culture which he found in
the older. Not that Lottie had not enjoyed remarkably
fine advantages for that time; she had read and learned
much more than she now understood; but knowledge
had, as yet, wrought no effectual work upon her—it had
not yet become a living principle; reflection had made
but little change in that youthful cheerfulness which
made her view every thing in the golden morning light
of her own warm feeling, and compelled her to idealize
as Schiller himself did, who, at that period, went so far
as to write of her: "A spirit like yours seeks things
that lie in the enchanted background, in a fairer light
than they really have; we seldom find such people
as you."

Her love for the poet awoke into powerful activity,
her desire to improve herself, as soon as the winter had
removed him again. She determined to be worthy of
him; and the manner in which, girl-like, she runs from
little things to great, makes an odd impression; in
one letter, jumping from Schiller to Gibbon, discussing
Christianity, leaving this to discourse of Plutarch, touching lightly on Pompey and Cæsar, turning from them to
the Portuguese and their merits in modern geographical
science, then bringing some new French romances under
review, and ending with Mirabeau.

In spite of this mosaic of subjects, however, the ripeness of her mind, in the sunshine of her love for a man so gifted, begins to be apparent in a multitude of fine and strikingly characteristic remarks and thoughts, unlike any thing seen in her before the earnestness of love brought her being to maturity. For example, she says: "The friendship that wants to share merely agreeable things is selfish;" at another place, "The heart can extract something from very small materials; the understanding, however, craves larger stores;" again, "Habit must be revered as one of the most beneficent of goddesses;" and, once more, "More is unquestionably gained by imparting our ideas to others than by merely bearing them round ourselves, for it is by communicating them that they receive clearness and sharpness."

And thus it went agreeably on. As her judgment acquired correctness respecting things, it grew noticeably surer respecting men; and we can well understand with what joy Schiller once proudly claimed this progress as the fruit of seeds planted by himself. In the autumn of 1788, he entered upon his professorship of history at Jena. This prevented a protracted interview with Charlotte the next summer; they merely met for a few days at Lauchstädt, and subsequently at Weimar. A declaration now took place, and, from that time forth, their correspondence assumes a liveliness and warmth which often moves us deeply, as it presents the great poet

on his most sympathetic and amiable side. And with
Lottie, too, there now comes to the foreground a passionate, boundless love, overshadowing all other thoughts,
so that even the reader of her letters experiences a sen-
sation of relief, when, at the close, he sees that the lovers
have reached the consummation of their wishes, and
formed that union which was to be to both the richest
spring of unbroken happiness during the sixteen years in
which they were to belong to each other, during all of
which our Lottie unfolded that devoted and abiding
loyalty and love of which only German women are
capable in so eminent a degree.

The obligation which the German nation owes to this
amiable woman becomes all the more manifest, when we
look at the change which his marriage wrought in the
poet. Down to that time he had not rightly apprehended
woman's nature ; all the female characters which he had
till then conceived—with the single exception of the remarkably portrayed violinist's wife in " Love and Intrigue "—have something hard and false ; they are
figures which, in spite of all their pathos, lack the true
warmth of life. We see that, till then, the poet had con-
templated women only through the medium of fantasy
or sense. From that time, on, he gives us a series of
noble female characters. Countess Terzky, the Duchess
of Friedland, Gustel von Blasewitz, Mary Stuart, Donna
Isabella, Agnes Sorel, the Maid of Orleans, Hedwig, Ger-
trude (Stauffacher's wife), can compare in life-likeness

with the creations of any other poet. There is in the relations of these women, to the men whom they loved, a truthfulness and a natural warmth (more especially in portraying the marriage relation) which, in Tell's wife, reaches the highest poetry; and which can be ascribed to the happiness of his home, and the influence of his Lottie.

Fr. Pecht del.   L Sichling sculp.

... ... The richest
... ...
... ...
... ...
his ... ...
eight... ... ...
paper, subseq... ... to receive it ... ...
and mean... ... ... and ... ...
where ... influence of ... ...

CHARLES MOOR.

(The Robbers.)

Our nature is the paper, and the world the envelope, which, together, constitute the perfect man. The complete personality is not merely the product of our native spiritual qualities and sensibilities. It is the result as well of the experiences which meet us in the course of life, the influences of the external world developing our personality, but, at the same time, transforming it, and making the result a complete character. The richest natures must, by the inevitable contact with life, be the more transformed in proportion as this contact is varied; and it is a great mistake to expect of a gifted man that, in his fiftieth year, he shall be exactly what he was in his eighteenth, when his life was an unwritten sheet of paper, subsequently to receive its coloring, and to be pale and mean, or brilliant and attractive. And those persons in whom the influence of the external world produces very slight changes, and whom we usually speak of as characters, are generally either meagre natures, or deficient in life.

In a soul as richly endowed as Schiller's was, the latter contingency is a thing impossible, since such a soul takes up into itself all the life of its times, lives it anew, and reflects it, as a diamond takes up the smallest beam of light, and breaks it into a thousand rays, while a whole world of sunshine can impart no splendor to the pebble. Although the attrition of the outer world brings its true value to the gem, and makes it continually more brilliant, it cannot change the worth of the pebble in the least; it can reduce its size, break it into fragments, but never enhance its value. Nor does it do so to frame it in costliest gold, while such a setting is recognized as simply due to the jewel.

It is, therefore, not to be wondered at, if the personality of the poet appears to us quite different at the outset of his life from what he was when his genius had matured and purified by the experiences of a rich inner and outer life. As his genius was the grandest and most awe-inspiring when it had advanced victoriously through life, it is a study all the more interesting to trace it back to its first work of power, as we find it in "The Robbers." Just as in the Bible, so in Schiller's play, the first quality that strikes us is power. In "The Robbers," we witness a struggle with the whole order of the world, carried on in the most energetic manner, and to just such an extent as this world was within the sphere of the poet's knowledge. That it was, at best, but a fragmentary acquaintance with the world; that Charles, with his great nature, could enter upon no better work than attacking defiantly an "ink-shedding age," going into the forests, becoming a robber-chief, and having melées with the police; this child-like want of relation between what was in his thought and the means which he took to reach his end; this shows us better than every thing how such fruit could ripen on the dusty seats of the Charles School at Stuttgart.

The irresistible effect which he wrought upon the youth of that time is explained by the extraordinary genius which the young poet expended in the effort to reach his odd goal. If Charles, in his stupid hunting-down of corpulent parsons and rich farmers, is like that giant who undertook to throw millstones to Spatzen; if he shows us in this, more distinctly than in any thing else, the horizon of the poet, which at that time extended only from Stuttgart to Ludwigsburg, he teaches us to comprehend the amazement which must have seized the cosmopolitan Goethe, as he looked upon this untrammelled production of the young man's genius, and the delight of all the youth, whose very soul was pictured in this wild life. And Charles differs merely from the youth of his time, that he was really able to hurl the millstones, and that he came soon enough to a confession of the folly with which he began his course. He says of himself:

"There he stands, poor fool! abashed and disgraced in the sight of Heaven; the boy that presumed to wield Jove's thunder, and overthrew pigmies when he should have crushed Titans."

Charles, in whom the poet draws his own portrait as

nowhere else, is, in what he says of his inner life, full already of that lofty spirit, that scorn for every thing common and low, that remained the most marked characteristic of Schiller's Muse, unchanged amid all his later transformations; and when the camp-life of the students and the robbers is subsequently portrayed in detail, there is brought into play a plastic power, which graves it all upon the memory, and makes it live. In spite of the continued blame with which we must visit all Charles's errors, when we are not compelled to smile at them, the heroic element in his character always takes us captive. In his gloomy humor, he sees only the shaded side of things, but this most clearly, as we learn from his genuinely student-life portrayal of the age, as well as from his own expression, that "the law never makes a great man." But that great men are appointed to make laws, not to overthrow them—this, twenty years and a fiery soul are not so well able to discern!

Inferior poets tell us that their hero is gifted, grand, imposing, even while he is doing very ordinary things; but Schiller's Charles is, to a certain extent, really so; in all that he says, there are traces of a remarkable man, in spite of his exaggerated feeling, his errors; even in spite of the sweltering pathos into which he is falling every minute.

Although the poet makes him fully confess his errors—

" Oh, fool that I was, to fancy that I could amend the world by misdeeds, and maintain law by lawlessness! I called it vengeance and equity; I presumed, O Providence, upon whetting the notches of Thy sword, and repairing Thy partialities; but—oh, vain trifling!—here I stand upon the brink of a fearful life, and learn with wailing and gnashing of teeth that *two men like myself could ruin the whole edifice of the moral world.* Pardon! pardon the boy who sought to forestall Thee; *to Thee alone belongeth vengeance.* Thou needest not the hand of man! But it is not in my power to recall the past. That which is ruin remains ruin; what I have thrown down will never more rise up again. Yet one thing is left me, whereby I may atone to the offended majesty of the law, and restore the order which I have violated"—

and so effects an undoing of the cruelties into which he had been hurried, step by step, through the fierce violence of youth ; yet we fear it is in this form a subsequent addition, a reflection put into the mouth of Charles by the poet when he revised the piece.

For the purposes of the artist, there are sufficient hints given in the play. At the very outset, he is represented as a lofty, proud, and massive figure ; and, on his subsequent visit to the castle of his fathers, Francis recognizes him by his wild, sun-burnt countenance, his long neck, his black, flashing eyes, and the dark, bushy eyebrows that overhang them. The scene in which we have represented him is the celebrated monologue, where, returning from his interview with Amelia, he thinks, in despair, of suicide, and whispers to himself :

" If the paltry pressure of this paltry thing " (putting a pistol to his head) " makes the wise man and the fool, the coward and the brave, the noble and the villain, equal " . . .

If Charles commits all possible cruelties, and reasons
sentimentally on them afterward, the discrepancy between his feelings and his actions is certainly not to
be solved; it lay in the mind of the poet, who wanted
to draw a character different from himself, and yet
transferred his own feelings and thoughts to his poetic
creation.

Fr. Pecht del.   A. Schultheiss sculp.

Amalia

Is it a poet's gift to portray what he has never known? We need not wonder if the youth, from the ... was unable to give in his first work her true ... to the only female figure introduced: if he does not reproduce her so faithfully as he does the wild companions of his youth — Roller, Schweizer, Spiegelberg, and others, whom he portrays from life ...

In Charles ... has painted himself rising in burning indignation against the order of things around him, a legalized condition of affairs that had settled into dead mechanical form. In Amelia on the other hand, whose features could hardly have been taken from a living original, we can see what ideas he had of noble women before he knew them. In a man of greatness, it is worth the trouble to examine the ... what indistinct and hastily-drawn features ... gives her ...

... of the elder Moor, early orphaned ... his house, and grew up ... the two brothers. It was but natural, therefore,

AMELIA.

Is a man able to portray what he has never known ?
If he cannot, we need not wonder if the youth, from the
Charles School, was unable to give in his first work her
true tint to the only female figure introduced; if he does
not represent her so faithfully as he does the wild companions of his youth — Roller, Schweizer, Spiegelberg,
and others, whom he portrayed from life.

In Charles, the poet has painted himself rising in
burning indignation against the order of things around
him, a legalized condition of affairs that had settled into
dead mechanical form. In Amelia, on the other hand,
whose features could hardly have been taken from
a living original, we can see what ideas he had of
noble women before he knew them In a man of his
greatness, it is worth the trouble to examine the somewhat indistinct and hastily-drawn features which he
gives her.

A poor niece of the elder Moor, early orphaned, she
was educated in his house, and grew up on equal footing
with the two brothers. It was but natural, therefore,

that, under these circumstances, her glowing, love-craving heart turned to the splendid character brought before her in the older brother. Even the envious Francis says of him :

> "Here, here Charles reigned sole monarch, like a god within his temple; he stood before thee, waking; he filled thy imagination, dreaming; the whole creation seemed to thee to centre in Charles, and to reflect him alone; it gave thee no other echo but of him."

In this all-victorious love, her enthusiastic soul goes wholly out to him, clings to him with unshakable fidelity, despite all the calumnies of the brother. She sees through these sooner than does the credulous father ; and steadfastly and courageously defends her lover. Love, that transforms us all, gives her, too, spirit and strength, makes her a heroine, teaches her to penetrate what is cunning, and despise what is base ; makes her know the round of all sensations, from those which are most blessed to those most fraught with death ; and gives her a wealth of experience that she had scarcely known before, for love is the school-mistress of woman.

This spirit, inspired by love, the timid girl preserves, and, with it, gallantly confronts the insidious brother, to whom, notwithstanding he holds her fate in his hand, she displays her scorn everywhere, and even tears the dagger from him when he persecutes her with his caresses, and puts the coward to flight. This touch is all the more fine and true, in that it makes more clear

to us the passionate desire of the cold Francis for her ;
for a woman of decision must have had a special charm
for a feeble-hearted spendthrift like himself; a weak
woman Francis would have recklessly misused and
trodden under foot.   Now, he can do no more than
break her heart by the news of Charles's death, brought
by Hermann, who had been tampered with by Francis,
and used merely as a tool.   The rich count cannot shake
her fidelity.   It is, however, brought into a state of
rarest perplexity when her lover, after years of separa-
tion, appears in the disguise of a stranger, and at once
takes her heart captive ; there being something in his
bearing which recalls the delightful days, long ago past,
with Charles.   The scene in which the artist has represented her, is where she conducts the stranger to the
portrait-gallery of her ancestors, sunk in painful recollections of her old happiness, so wonderfully connected
with the experience of the present moment, as she shows
Charles's likeness to the stranger, and asks a solution of
the riddle written in his face.   He has conceived of
Amelia as a slim, tall figure, with great, dark, enthusiastic
eyes, full lips, indicative of longing and tenderness, a lofty
brow quivering with pain; and, putting the bitter question to fate—why all the charm of her life must be with-
drawn.   Her own words express best what she would say :

"Gone ! as our best joys perish.   Whatever lives, lives to die in sorrow.
We engage our hearts, and grasp after the things of this world, only to undergo
the pang of losing them."

The hot eagerness, exaggeration, reckless passion which breathes through all that Schiller wrote, during this first period, pulsates also in Amelia as often—and that is almost always—as she thinks of her love, whether lamenting him, whom she believes to be dead, or surrendering herself to the recollection of past days :

> " His warm embrace—oh, ravishing delight!
> With heart to heart the fiery pulses dance—
> Our every sense wrapped in ecstatic night,
> Our souls in blissful harmony entranced.
>
> He's gone! forever gone! Alas! in vain
> My bleeding heart in bitter anguish sighs ;
> To me is left alone this world of pain, ·
> And mortal life in hopeless sorrow dies."

or whether, with a feeling of dread, she at last discloses these sensations to the stranger :

> " ' You are in tears, Amelia ?' these were his very words—and spoken with such expression—such a voice ! Oh! it summoned up a thousand dear remembrances !—scenes of past delight, as in my youthful days of happiness, my golden spring-tide of love. The nightingales sang again with the same sweetness, the flowers breathed the same delicious fragrance as when I used to hang enraptured on his neck. Ha! false, perfidious heart! dost thou seek thus artfully to veil thy perjury ?"

Incredible as this not recognizing him is, inasmuch as directly after she knows him at once in the forest, there is at least more consistency in her conduct than in Charles, who, in every situation, merely obeys the impulse of the moment, while she never forgets her

passion—always speaks and acts conformably to it; in
her last interview, even wishing to die in her rapture:

"I have him; O ye stars, I have him! His forever; he forever, ever mine!
O ye Heavenly Powers, support me in this ecstasy of bliss, lest I sink beneath
its weight!

" *Charles.* Tear her from my neck! kill her! kill him, kill me, yourselves,
everybody! Let the whole world perish!   [*About to rush off.*

"*Amelia.* Whither? What? Love! Eternity! Happiness! Never-ending joys!
and thou wouldst fly?

" *Charles.* Away! away! most unfortunate of brides. See with thine own
eyes; ask and hear it with thine own ears! Most miserable of fathers! Let
me escape hence forever!

"*Amelia.* Support me! For Heaven's sake, support me! It is growing
dark before my eyes! He flies!"

or when, seized with horror at his and her condition,
she begs her death at his hands:

' Oh! for Heaven's sake! By all that is merciful! I ask no longer for love.
I know that our stars fly from each other in opposition. Death is all I ask."

Fr. Pecht del.

J. L. Raab sculp.

Franz Moor

... mild, dry, wooden" Francis, his own father ... venomous reptile, whose fearful character will probably always be regarded as one of the greatest creations of our poet. This appellation seems to have ... proverbially common in the Moor mansion, to indicate the ... of the ... son, before his cha...

neither ... ... ness; his inclin... to ... his most marked characte... ; he ... a strong philosophic bend, and everywh... indicates his close acquaintance with the materialist philosophy of the seventeenth and eighteenth centuries ... he has appropriated ... method, and used ... in justification of his horrible wishes.

Men are, cont... more inclined to ...

FRANCIS MOOR.

(*The Robbers.*)

As the "cold, dry, wooden" Francis, his own father speaks of the venomous reptile, whose fearful character will probably always be regarded as one of the greatest creations of our poet. This appellation seems to have become proverbially common in the Moor mansion, to indicate the younger of the two sons, before his character was better known.

We see, in the very first scene, that he was lacking neither in wit nor in wickedness—least of all in reflectiveness; his inclination to sophistry and craft is his most marked characteristic; he has a strong philosophic bend, and everywhere indicates his close acquaintance with the materialistic philosophy of the seventeenth and eighteenth centuries; he has appropriated its entire method, and used it in justification of his horrible wishes.

Men are, confessedly, more inclined to envy the brilliant external qualities of others than their internal traits. The existence of these they find it more con-

venient to deny. The striking splendor of the older
brother's nature, exerting, as it did, a magic charm over
every one, filled the younger with such a hatred of
nature, which seemed so neglectful of him, as to make
him forget even the ties of blood. This wild rebellion
against nature becomes the ground-thought of his being,
and he frankly confesses it when he says:

"No small cause have I for being dissatisfied with Dame Nature, and, by
mine honor, I will have amends. Why has she heaped on me this burden of
deformity? on me especially, just as if she had spawned me from her refuse!
Why to me, in particular, this snub of the Laplander, these Negro lips, these
Hottentot eyes?"

The artist has only to complete the hints which are
given here, to perfect the representation of Francis, who
represents himself with so little flattery; he must give
him that knavish, externally composed, inwardly passionate appearance; he must indicate that tendency to
reflect, develop the hidden, secret brooding of his character, as these qualities manifest themselves throughout
the play. His is the nature of a recluse; let his wishes
and passions be of the wildest kind, his nervous temperament always leaves him in the lurch when he needs
courage. Cowardice and cruelty are cousins which
almost always appear together, and this is the case
with Francis. He is a pale, red-haired, overgrown
youngster, with thin, pale lips, who never can look one
in the face; a tall young man of twenty, with an un-
formed, boyish face, in which only the forehead is broad

and powerful, the rest weak and incomplete. Francis is vain, and therefore richly clothed, although the incessant agitation going on within him makes him neglectful of his toilet. Even in his wildest passion, he must maintain a distinguished appearance; the nest-bird of an old family cannot avoid the delicate and effeminate conventionalities of life. Be he lacking in spirit, there is no want of mind, acumen, and fancy; and even where he has not at hand all the resources he needs, his active imagination is perpetually causing him to exaggerate his strength:

"Let those swim who can, the heavy may sink. To me she gave naught else; and how to make the best use of my endowment is my present business. Men's natural rights are equal; claim is met by claim, effort by effort, and force by force. Right is with the strongest; the limits of our power constitute our laws."

The foundation of his education, the materialistic philosophy of the eighteenth century, displays itself particularly in all his reasonings on the conscience:

"Honor! truly a very convenient coin, which those who know how to pass it may lay out to very good advantage. Conscience! oh, yes, a useful scarecrow to frighten sparrows away from cherry-trees; it is something like a fairly-written bill of exchange, with which your bankrupt merchant staves off the evil day.

"Then, courage, and onward! The man who fears nothing is as powerful as he who is feared by everybody."

In like manner, where he makes merry with the ties of blood:

"He is thy father! He gave thee life; thou art his flesh and blood, and therefore he must be sacred to thee. Again a most inconsequential deduction. Do I then owe him thanks for his affection? Why, what is it but a piece of vanity, the

6

besetting sin of the artist who admires his own works, however hideous they may
be ? Look you! this is the whole juggle wrapped up in a mystic veil, to work on
our fears ; and shall I, too, be fooled like an infant ? "

Or where he justifies the murder of his father:

" Is my soaring spirit to be chained down to the snail's pace of matter?
To blow out a wick that is already flickering upon its last drop of oil—'tis
nothing more."

Thinking so lightly of the murder of his own father,
of course that of his brother is the merest trifle :

" A happy journey to you; brother! The spleeny, gouty moralist of a conscience
may trouble old usurers on their death-bed ; he will never gain audience with me."

To complete the portrait, there is only wanting sensuality, since this and cruelty always go together.

The closing scenes, in which the despised conscience
at last maintains its rights, and scourges the poor Francis,
are of fearful power, and develop with the utmost clearness the whole wealth of Schiller's genius. After seeing
this abandoned man seek all the arguments to build the
superstructure of his crime upon, it thrills us to witness
his own destruction beneath the crumbling ruins of his
own edifice:

" Vulgar prejudice, mere superstition! It has not yet been proved that the past
is not past and forgotten, or that there is an Eye above this earth. To die! Why
does that word frighten me thus ? To give an account to the Avenger there, above
the stars ! And if He should be just—the wail of orphans and widows, of the.
oppressed and tormented, ascending to His ears, and He be just ? Why have they
been afflicted, and why have I been permitted to trample upon them?

" There is no God. I am well aware that those who have come off short in this
world, look forward to eternity ; but they will be sadly disappointed. I have always

read that our whole being is nothing more than a blood-spring, and that with its last drop mind and thought dissolve into nothing. But I do not wish to be immortal. Let them be so that like. I have no wish to hinder them. I will force Him to annihilate me. I will so provoke His fury that He may utterly destroy me. Tell me which are the greatest sins, which excite Him to the utmost wrath.

"Listen to my prayer, O God in heaven! It is the first time; it shall never happen again. Hear me, God in heaven. O Lord, I have been no common murderer; I have been guilty of no petty crimes, gracious Lord; I cannot pray. Here! and here [*striking his breast and his forehead*]! all is so void—so barren! [*Rises from his knees.*] No, I will not pray. Heaven shall not have that triumph nor hell that pastime."

This gradual increase of the horror of death is painted with all the more power, from the very psychological truthfulness of the monster strangling himself out of the very fear of death.

Fiesco

FIESCO.

(The Conspiracy of Fiesco.)

THE three earliest plays of Schiller grow out of a reaction against the existing order of things; they are characterized by a revolutionary spirit. In "The Robbers," where society is attacked, this has the freest play. In "Fiesco," it limits itself to revolt against the State; in "Love and Intrigue," it has for its object differences in social rank.

Fiesco was intended to be a "republican tragedy;" in it Schiller wanted to make an apotheosis of that form of government. Under his hands, however, it became something quite different—almost the reverse; for the most of the characters which he portrays—Gianettino Doria, the Moor, Sacco, Calcagno—are nothing but adopted citizens of a republic; and even their preferred representative, Verrina, with his cold, empty, conventional Roman spirit, is not able to make their possibility intelligible to us; in short, the poet's genius, while instinctively grasping what is true, was not sufficiently acquainted with the world to insure correctness. There is, in the play, many a reminder of Coriolanus, Julius Cæsar, Emilia, Galotti ; Julia, Verrina, and the Moor, are old acquaintances.

Original as Fiesco himself is, even in what we must regard as misconceived, we are compelled to recognize everywhere the lion's claw. How perfect are the popular scenes ! How extremely rich in invention, in unexpected incidents, in thrilling, captivating passages, the whole play ! How happily, and with what a genial instinct, is the national coloring brought to light in the hero !

Fiesco is wholly an Italian, an aristocrat, and a politician. He has his nation's fluency, and love of talk ; he has the craft and secrecy, the presence of mind, and quick perception, of his countrymen ; colossal and imposing in character, he has the immoderate pride of the genuine aristocrat, and a little vanity in the enjoyment of his own brilliant personal qualities. The boundless ambition which consumes him is conjoined with a love of intrigue, but, at the same time, with so much scorn of danger, as to win our interest and sympathy.

The most remarkable trait of the character is, however, the manner in which the young poet brings political affairs to light in Fiesco ; we have an instance of this in the scene where the artist represents him in his interview with the citizens :

"The government was democratical, every thing was subjected to a majority. The cowards were more numerous than the brave. Numbers prevailed."

Swarthy, with cunning, penetrating, snake-like eyes; slim and tall, flexible and agile as a panther; especially characteristic is his imposing bearing, which affects all, winning for him the hearts of women as well as of the people; in short, of all who want to be captivated, not convinced; and not, without truth, can he say of himself, "The blind of Genoa know my step." The mysterious background, that impenetrability of his, which all the women, as well as the statesmen, recognize in him, increases his power; for, like every hidden thing, it only creates an eager curiosity. It does not speak well for human nature, but it is true, notwithstanding, that open spirits, secure in their own good intent, do not, however gifted, exert that influence on the masses which cunning politicians wield. At the foundation of this there may be a true instinct, that with all the ability of these straight-forward souls to comprehend large plans, they may not be able to bring them to completion, since the doing of all great deeds is veiled from the world.

But that which especially charms us in Fiesco is the richness and inexhaustibility of his nature. His culture, spirit, manly beauty, nimble wit and grace, fire and courage—these are all united in him, charming not only the weak and susceptible, but showing those of keen perceptions that he was a man called to high deeds.

The individuality of his nature appears most remark-ably in his humorous relations to the Moor, since there he moves the freest. The Moor is a droll rascal; and

gifted men like Fiesco are often captivated by wit. This
appears strikingly in the beginning of their acquaintance,
where the Moor leads off with the assertion that he is
an honorable man, an assurance that becomes suspicious
the oftener it is repeated. It is characteristic of the
Moor that he is willing to be called a knave, but not
a blockhead; and this draws Fiesco to him. Their
relations are also indicated by Fiesco's reply, when a
Jesuit said that a fox lay disguised there in sheep's
clothing: "One fox smells out another." The cavalier
in Fiesco is expressed, when, speaking of his name,
he said:

"Blockhead! that name is as easy to be remembered as it was difficult to
achieve. · Has Genoa more such names than one ?"

Or in his vexation that he must be praised by a knave,
he breaks out into the sentence now classical:

"The Moor has done his work. The Moor may go."

Such an expression would easily please a youthful
poet.

Fiesco's relation to Verrina is very finely conceived.
As a riper, larger, more richly‑endowed nature, he
towers far above him; and yet that unbending strength
of character awes him, because he feels that his more
elastic constitution has no power against it. They love
each other, because each has what the other wants; yet,
in this feeling, Fiesco is, perhaps, the more truthful and
noble, because with him this sentiment springs from

genuine regard ; while, in Verrina, it has its basis in hope and admiration.

Here, it must be confessed, we come to the goal of our admiration, and are compelled to confess that the execution is not equal to the conception. Especially open to criticism is Fiesco's relation to the two women who love him, the heartlessness with which he treats them both, his brutality to Julia Imperiali, his calculated coldness to Leonore. The tortuous character of his political dialectics stands in wonderful contrast to the conduct which is assumed to grow from his reasoning. To what purpose does Fiesco represent to himself that shame diminishes with the increase of sin, and that it is an act of unparalleled greatness to steal a crown, although he can quietly confess to himself that the Genoese are no republicans, and that he is the man who should be at their head? Not less repellant is the braggart tone that here and there breaks out, smacking altogether too much of student's renowning, and strongly contrasted with the great delicacy and grace which he commonly displays. These inequalities characterize the transition period in which the poet then was; there is insecurity in the artistic use of all his materials. In "Love and Intrigue" it came, if possible, more prominently into view, to disappear in "Don Carlos," before his well-won skill. The weakness, in handling his theme, appears particularly in the fifth act, which is decidedly inferior to those preceding it. It awakens sensations

7

of extremely varied character; and is all the less satisfactory from the fact, that in it the poet dropped what
is probable, although elsewhere, with all his wealth of
invention, he clung to it.   A pathos carried even to
wearisome lengths blinds us to his noble style, whose
suggestiveness and power charm us even in earlier
portions of the same play.

Leonora.

LEONORA.

(*The Conspiracy of Fiesco.*)

ALTHOUGH it is not to be denied that the characters of
"Fiesco" have something of exaggeration in almost every
one of them, that they partake of the transcendentalism
of youth, and, at times, even of its want of moderation
and its crudeness, yet this reproach can be brought least
of all against Countess Lavagna, in whom the young poet
has, for the first time, succeeded in portraying a woman
who awakes our warmest interest. She is a sweet,
gentle, and yet passionate creation, wholly given to
tenderness ; and yet, in her bitterest grief, throwing it
off, out of fear that the sight of her sorrow may occasion one sad moment to her adored husband. Fiesco
was her first love—her whole heaven lay in him, and
she rejoiced ever in her triumph in having conquered
him :

"A blooming Apollo, blending the manly beauty of Antinous ! Such was his
noble and majestic deportment, as if the illustrious state of Genoa rested alone
upon his youthful shoulders. . . . Ah ! Arabella, how we devoured those looks !
With what anxious envy did every one count those directed to her companions !
They fell among us like the golden apple of discord ; tender eyes burned

fiercely, soft bosoms beat tumultuously ; jealousy burst asunder all our bonds of friendship.

"And now to call him mine! Giddy, wondrous fortune! To call the pride of Genoa mine! He who from the chisel of the exhaustless artist, Nature, sprang forth all perfect, combining every virtue of his sex in the most perfect union!" . . .

and now, married but a brief half-year, she must contemplate the possibility of losing this priceless possession; in her own house she sees the man of her heart trifling in wanton gallantry with another, and heaping attentions upon her, which increase her jealousy tenfold. From the conversation between Calcagno and Sacco, we learn how the world looked upon her rigid code of morals, and the relation in which her husband stood to Imperiali :

" *Calcagno.* They say she is a pattern of the strictest virtue.

" *Sacco.* They lie! She is the whole volume on that insipid text, Calcagno ; thou must choose one or the other—either to give up thy heart or thy profession.

" *Calcagno.* The count is faithless to her; and of all the arts that may seduce a woman, the subtlest is jealousy. A plot against the Dorias will, at the same time, occupy the count, and give me easy access to his house. Thus, while the shepherd guards against the wolf, the fox shall make havoc of the poultry."

While we are learning the plans of the debauchee with reference to her, we see, at the same time, out of what pitiful material the stubborn Verrina purposes to construct the edifice of a Roman republic of the elder time.

The artist has represented Leonora in the first scene, where her whole character comes most distinctly into view; he has portrayed her enthusiasm for her husband,

and the elegiac thrill that runs through her whole frame
when, tearing off the mask, she throws herself into the
chair, and yet is able to find scarcely any thing but
words of admiration for him.

But if she has no weapons save tears against him
whom she loves, yet she is too much a woman, she has
too much spirit, not to find the most crushing words to
hurl at her hated rival; she listens to Julia scarcely two
minutes, before distinctly seeing that Fiesco cannot love
such a woman:

> "Congratulate me, girl! It is impossible I can have lost my Fiesco; or, if
> I have, the loss must be but trifling."

She replies with a sharpness which stood more at
the command of women of her stamp than at that of
most men:

> "Poor husband! *Here*, a blooming beauty smiles upon him; *there*, he is
> nauseated by a peevish sensibility. Signora, signora, for God's sake, consider; if
> he have not lost his understanding, which will he choose?
> "*Leonora.* You, madame, if he has lost it."

But if she publicly admits the victory of her rival, if
she relinquishes her claim to her lover, yet the mere view
of his medallion in Julia's hands brings her completely
to herself again, and shows that her love has not been
lessened.

Pain embitters and despoils common natures; higher
ones it exalts. Our Leonora belongs to the last, and
therefore Calcagno finds, exactly at the instant that seems

most favorable to him, that he had misled himself in
reckoning upon her undeception :

"I understand thee—thou thoughtest my wounded pride would plead in thy
behalf. Thou didst not know that she who loves Fiesco feels even the pang, that
rends her heart, ennobling. Begone! Fiesco's perfidy will not make Calcagno rise
in my esteem; but will lower humanity."

The almost idolatrous love with which Leonora is
filled appears everywhere, but most of all in the turbulent
flow and reflow of feeling; in that "joyful, sorrowful,
and thoughtful" state, which makes the wife of seven
months blush like a timid girl, when the waiting-woman
brings her husband's greetings to her; but, in the next
moment, her doubts return; she will abandon him, she
will load him with reproaches; and yet she cannot go
further than to utter a gentle lament :

"To be your wife was more than I deserved, but she who was your wife
deserved at least respect. How bitter is the tongue of Calumny! How the wives
and maidens of Genoa now look down upon me! 'See,' they say, 'how droops
the haughty one, whose vanity aspired to Fiesco!'"

In saying, so tenderly and touchingly, that she can
never hate him, she only proves herself to be of German
birth. Had Schiller known the women of Italy, he would
scarcely have represented her as comforting herself so
easily; he would hardly have put into the mouth of an
Italian wife the words :

"He directs, and I obey. Why should I fear? And yet I tremble, Arabella,
and my heart beats fearfully with apprehension. For Heaven's sake, damsels, do
not leave me!"

German, too, is the touch where, after Fiesco had procured for her completest triumph over her rival, Leonora pleads in her behalf, instead of enjoying her downfall ; German, too, her jealousy of her husband's authority :

" Here is no choice but evil. Unless he gain the ducal power, Fiesco perishes. If I embrace the duke, I lose my husband."

And, with a fine instinct for her own happiness, she becomes a republican, because she feels at once that if she does not lose her husband on the way to the throne, she will surely lose him on the throne itself. But when the contest has once broken out, she has no longer a thought except of her love ; the fear of the woman is utterly extinguished by the power of her passion :

" No—my hero shall embrace a heroine."

At his side she will either conquer or die. The last is her fate. Such boundless, overwhelming feeling, while at the side of a husband, not now able to reciprocate it wholly, must lead to tragic results ; but that she should be murdered by Fiesco himself, while in her fatal disguise, is needless cruelty, which tortures our feelings, and which, probably, rather springs from misused Shakespearian reminiscences, than from Schiller's own heart.

Fr Pecht del.   J. Jaquenot sculp.

Andrew Doria

... ... and in voluntary subjection to organic laws, whether of the State or of art.

The progress which Schiller made in advancing from ... ... of "The Robbers" to an historical theme ... ... unquestionable, ... was compelled to ... ... his characters with a firmer hand, restrain his ... ... fancy, give them a local coloring, keep them within natural limits, and so, step by step mature his most perfect works. It is true "Fiesco" is a first attempt to accommodate himself to the demands of historical material, and, on the whole, his success has not been great. There is the same wildness as, if not a greater than, that which repels us in "The Robbers"

ANDREW DORIA.

(*The Conspiracy of Fiesco.*)

By freedom, youth generally understands license, immoderation, or a kind of good-natured anarchy, whereas it really consists in the absence of all arbitrary authority, and in voluntary subjection to organic laws, whether of the State or of art.

The progress which Schiller made in advancing from the monstrous figures of " The Robbers " to an historical theme is, therefore, unquestionable, since he was compelled to draw his characters with a firmer hand, restrain his luxuriant fancy, give them a local coloring, keep them within natural limits, and so, step by step, mature his most perfect works. It is true " Fiesco " is a first attempt to accommodate himself to the demands of historical material; and, on the whole, his success has not been great. There is the same wildness as, if not a greater than, that which repels us in " The Robbers," and yet there is a lack of that creative power that we find in the earlier play. From the roughness that was natural to his theme, we often come to a hollow pathos,

like the imitated ostensibly old Roman republicanism of
the play—a thing that has no real place in the world,
because there is nothing of it; it has no body; it is a
mere phantom—a sham.   Its representative, Verrina,
with all his wild and genuine energy, yet from a want
of all positive ideas, insists upon really nothing ; he
continually cries "freedom," but he gives us no explana-
tion of the sense which he ascribes to this very indefinite
word.   Verrina's conventional Roman republicanism unquestionably indicates the horizon of the fiery poet at
that time; and it is extremely interesting to trace the
formlessness of the political ideas in his first three plays,
the increase of definiteness and exactness in "Don Carlos,"
and, at last, their complete wholeness in "Tell."   What a
difference in the mode of treatment, while the same
effort to reach the truth lies at the basis of all! what
noble wisdom in the words of the dying Attinghausen,
and the demands of the Swiss peasantry, compared with
the chaotic confusion in " Fiesco ! "

The want of culture, which he later so completely
filled in his "Don Carlos" and "Tell," once granted, we
are compensated partly by the dramatic power displayed
in the whole treatment of the theme—partly by the
majestic greatness of some of his characters.   To endow
a figure with greatness of soul, and yet to preserve its
individuality, is the work of an artist who is himself
great.   That Schiller could do this in Andrew Doria, and
that, too, with a few master-strokes, speaks more loudly in

favor of his genuine artistic skill than all the rest of the play. Men do not recognize greatness of soul so much directly, as in comparing man with man, and in noticing the magical influence that it works. This influence of the old hero is everywhere displayed with the greatest delicacy in the play; everywhere we meet the respect that is paid him—either in the form of timidity or reverence. Thus, Leonora herself, that fine womanly nature, says, at the very moment when she dreams and wishes for the downfall of his family, that it is superfluous for him to be good, for he is gentle, and, at the same time, great. Doria is always the first thought in the mind of every man; whether with reverence or hate, they all must think of him. Fiesco calls his gentleness more dreadful than the defiance of his nephew; Verrina calls his chains silken ones; addresses the most glowing panegyric to him, and sharply discriminates between good statesmanship and that evil kingcraft that, under all circumstances, requires restraint. When Doria himself speaks, his first thought is of justice; his second of love for the state. In reproaching his nephew for seeking to destroy his country, he gives him, in ten words, a very sound lesson in politics, although he discloses to us a weakness that we do not find amiss in him—a too great love for his kinsmen; a quality repugnant to us in men without merit; and yet, regarded as a sign of goodness of heart—a touching quality in an old hero. The greatness of his character comes first into

view in the manner in which he demeans himself in time
of danger, and disarms his adversary by magnanimity,
when he says to Fiesco :

"Lavagna, your fate resembles mine; benevolence is rewarded with ingratitude.
The Moor informs me of a plot; I send him back to you in chains, and shall sleep
to-night without a guard."

The tumult having broken out, and the adversary
not being willing to be outwitted, but warning him to
fly, yet without allowing Doria to suspect that Fiesco
was he who gave this counsel, Andrew answers calmly :

"Fiesco has a noble mind; I never injured him, and he will not betray me.

"*Fiesco.* Fiesco has a noble mind, and yet betrays thee. He gives thee proof
of both.

"*Andrew.* There is a guard which would defy Fiesco's power, unless he led
against them legions of spirits.

"*Fiesco [scornfully].* That guard I should be glad to see, to dispatch it with a
message for eternity.

"*Andrew [in an elevated manner].* Vain scoffer, knowest thou not that Andrew
has seen his eightieth year, and that Genoa, beneath his rule, is happy ?"

His lofty confidence, which springs from a good
conscience, is, nevertheless, betrayed; yet, in his grief
over the deception, he remains. none the less imposing;
he thrills us, whether he says to the German body-guard :

"Hark! Germans, hark! These are the Genoese, whose chains I broke. Do
your countrymen thus recompense their benefactors? . . . Save yourselves—
leave me; and go, declare the horrid story to the shuddering nations, that Genoa
slew its father!"—

or whether, after vanquishing his adversaries, he begs of
the Genoese a place to die :

" Go, make it known through Genoa that Andrew Doria is still alive. Say that Andrew entreats the citizens, his children, not to drive him, in his old age, to dwell with foreigners, who ne'er would pardon the exalted state to which he raised his country. Say this—and farther say, that Andrew begs but so much ground within his fatherland as may contain his bones."

His words worked powerfully at last. Not · only does half Genoa run—at least, after Fiesco's death—to Andrew, but even Verrina feels himself compelled, after seeing the mistake which he had made in the character of his countrymen and Fiesco, to turn to him as to the firmest pillar of Genoa's freedom.

Fr.Pecht del.

A.Fleischmann sculp.

Julia Imperiali

JULIA IMPERIALI.

(The Conspiracy of Fiesco.)

IF Schiller has succeeded in giving to Countess Lavagna all the melting tenderness and charm of a finely-toned nature, his treatment of the Countess Imperiali is all the more unfortunate. Not simply that he represents her coarse and flippant in a degree which is not common, even in ladies several stages lower in the scale of society, but he endows her besides with a not inconsiderable love of applause, blended with stupidity, and crowns her character with an excess of haughtiness and mystery.

That the sister of Gianettino Doria—that pattern of a profligate spendthrift—should not be exactly a model of amiability, is not improbable ; but her coarseness smacks rather of studies pursued at Stuttgart than in Genoa. Her language, compared with the wonderful refinement of Fiesco, is like that of a braggart student roaring through all the streets, compared with the finish of a diplomat of the old school. Is it any less than this when

she says to Fiesco, in whose very house she is received
as a guest :

"Jealousy, jealousy! Poor thing! what would she wish for [*admiring herself
in the glass*]? Could she desire a higher compliment than were I to declare her
taste mine own [*haughtily*]? Doria and Fiesco! Would not the Countess of
Lavagna have reason to feel honored, if Doria's niece deigned to envy her choice?"

Where such haughtiness is exhibited by the representative of sovereignty, it ought not to be taken ill that
thoughts of revolt are current.

And yet this high-spirited heart is sensitive to love,
and has genuine sensibility. But if love and good
fortune make noble natures still grander, they intoxicate
lower ones ; they make evil qualities still worse. And
so our fair Julia, when believing herself secure in
Fiesco's love, is tortured with a real lust of vainglory,
and, longing for vengeance, she hurries from her home
to enjoy without delay her triumph over her opponent.
It is a remarkable phenomenon, that members of the
fair sex, however great their *esprit du corps*, yet have
almost, without exception, very little good-will one to
another, and pass their judgments with a correctness
that is amazing, in view of the little inclination felt
toward each other. And thus the coarse Julia soon
discovers, of herself, that a less sensitive, a more coquet-
tish and witty nature would better suit the perfidious
Fiesco, and in this she is probably right; but Leonora
finds much sooner that these qualities are by no means
marked in Julia. As the ladies speak their minds to

each other without much circumlocution, it is but
natural that they part without any excess of mutual
tenderness, and become mortal enemies. But, with the
hot blood of an Italian woman, such an enmity not
unfrequently leads to the attempt to make away with a
rival; and, three hundred years ago, when poison was
much more common than now, such a step was easily
taken. Fiesco's horror, when he learns this proof of
Julia's love to him—for it is nothing else—seems to us,
therefore, a little German. Perhaps, however, it is a
studied gallantry, by which Fiesco moves the fair
countess to come to him ; the wanton casuistry con-
veyed in the lines—

"The senses should always be blind messengers, and not know the secret
compact between nature and fancy"—

would scarcely have touched a lady of high or low
degree, least of all would it have brought her to the
house of the speaker.

In like manner, it is a little improbable that the hot-
blooded, sensuous Julia should deliver such long speeches
about her position as :

"Thy countenance is as glowing as thy words. Ah! and my own, too, burns
with guilty fire. Hence, I entreat thee, hence; let us seek the light—the tempting
darkness might lead astray the excited senses, and, in the absence of the modest
day, might stir them to rebellion. Haste, I conjure thee, leave this solitude !

"If I betray the safeguards of my honor, that thou mayst cover me with shame
at will, what have I less to lose than all ? Wouldst thou know more, scoffer?
Shall I confess that the whole secret wisdom of our sex is but a sorry precaution

9

for the defence of this weak fortress, which, in the end, is the sole object of assault by all your vows and protestations; and which (I blush to own it) is so willingly surrendered—so often betrayed to the enemy upon the first wavering of virtue!"

By having such thoughts at that time, she shows much more intellect, and much less tact, than an Italian lady would ordinarily exhibit; and speaks in the tone of a German professor: There is more truth and nature in her words when she says:

"Hear, Fiesco, one word more. When we know our virtue to be in safety, we are heroines; in its defence, no more than children [*fixing her eyes on him wildly*]; furies, when we avenge it. Hear me! Shouldst thou strike me to the heart with coldness?"

In the highest degree unknightly is the vengeance which she resolves upon. It is of a repugnant coarseness; no man of honor, least of all an Italian cavalier, who, with all his villany, cannot be denied to have some refinement in this respect, would do thus to a woman who, however great her fault may have been, had sinned out of sheer love to him. If her brother is more than ungallant, and declares his desire "for a piece of woman's flesh done up in a great, great patent of nobility," it may be not incorrect. Brothers have a right over all the world to be ungallant, and it must be confessed that it is fully justified, because, at best, they are mere make-shifts, stop-gaps; but the lover, even when simulating passion, is never justified in such rude treatment of her who, at last, and amid all changes of circumstance, is to be the victim of his own knavish malice. This touch of crudeness and coarseness only shows the bewilderment in which Schiller's ideas then were, and that lack of delicacy in the forms of social converse, which the Suabians had then, and have now, in a measure ; a little of which may have clung to our young poet, at a time when his relations with women had not extended far beyond the famous baker's wife.

FERDINAND

Not only the .... lives, and receives impressions .... dations and .... we would .... ction with ....ruption of morals and the .... little ..ugh during the last century, ... compr..hend the motive of "Love and .... understand how this play could have called .... a mighty echo in Germany. The insecure and .... condition of the poet himself, at that time, ... taken into account if we want to understand the .... into being while Schiller was .... by ...al persecution, which lay like a heavy .... upon his .... and completed after a ...... from the clutch of a ...... which knew no .... except the .... which hemmed .. in, "Love and Intrigue" must nece..- sarily bear witness ... Schiller's revolt from ... political

FERDINAND.

(Love and Intrigue.)

Not only the time in which an artist lives, and receives impressions, but also his personal relations and humors when he wrote, must be studied, if we would know the quality of his work.

We have already hinted at this in connection with Louisa. Without recalling the thorough corruption of morals and the absolutism prevailing in little courts during the last century, the reader does not comprehend the motive of "Love and Intrigue," nor understand how this play could have called out such a mighty echo in Germany. The insecure and troubled condition of the poet himself, at that time, is to be taken into account, if we want to understand the piece. Springing into being while Schiller was oppressed by ducal persecution, which lay like a heavy burden upon his great soul, and completed after a flight from the clutch of a tyranny which knew no bounds, except the geographical ones which hemmed it in, "Love and Intrigue" must necessarily bear witness to Schiller's revolt from the political

condition of his country, a revolt only too well justified
in the end, strange as it may seem to us to-day.

Repulsive to us as is the chaotic character of this
play, we are all the more amazed at the power of the
poet, that really superhuman glow and force with which
he bears us on, and compels us to be partakers even of
his own errors. Our feelings are overborne by him, even
when our understanding and taste perfectly perceive the
crudeness of his picture, and the want of all fine and
compensatory shades. This rawness lies much more in
the execution, quite beyond the reach of this young,
little experienced, fiery artist, than in the comprehension
of the entire plan, which is as severely truthful as the
sketches of the characters are lifelike. It. is only the
want of nice detail that makes the *dramatis personæ* so
monstrous ; and, therefore, the secondary characters,
who need detail less — the violinist, with his lively
musician's nature, and the stupid, prattling mother—are
masterly drawn, because here a sketch is all that is
wanted.

The peculiar loftiness of soul which Schiller displays
everywhere, reconciles us to the above deficiencies, and
all the more that they are genuinely national; we see in
them the Suabian traits of the poet clearer than anywhere else in his works. Penurious of words as the
Suabian is, when excited and compelled to muster up
his forces, he has a certain nervous eloquence. The
fanatical, enthusiastic, reckless passionateness in the

Suabian character, as well as its stiff obstinacy, Schiller
has painted with extreme skill in his Ferdinand ; and
revolting as is the student-like boasting of this young
man, we must, at least, confess that it is all the more
genuinely characteristic that there is nothing insincere in
it, but that it exhibits the unbounded glow and unre-
straint of a youth of profound sensibility, and no little
unapproachableness.

The same consuming fire which he infused into his
Ferdinand coursed through the poet's own veins, as
we can easily see from scattered letters of his, which
have come down from his youth, where an excess of hot
passion breaks out at every occasion. If Goethe, in his
Tasso, Werter, Clàvigo, and Weisslingen, has portrayed
some sides of his own character, Schiller has certainly
not done less in his Ferdinand. In this nature, open
to the gentlest and tenderest touches of feeling, and the
next instant blazing up like powder, in this unconsciously
glowing soul, in this purity of heart, in the exquisite
sensibility of the character, in the unwillingness to give
way to conviction, or to be silenced by the voice of the
world — who does not recognize in this the medical
student of the Stuttgart school?

The sharp and battle-loving quality of Ferdinand's
nature is not less note-worthy. If those characters
from Goethe, which we have mentioned above, display
something feminine, in Schiller we feel stimulated and
refreshed by the thoroughly manly nerve which, in

Ferdinand, carries us back to the student's wild
energy.

Nowhere has the poet displayed this native manli-
ness and natural strength in such sharp antagonism to a
poor, nerveless, weakly soul, as in Chief-Marshal Kalb.
The contrast is presented where the major confronts the
marshal with these words:

"*Ferdinand.* Marshal, this letter must have dropped out of your pocket on
parade, and I have been the fortunate finder. . . . Read it, read it. If I am not
good enough for a lover, perhaps I may do for a pimp.

'*Marshal.* Confusion!

"*Ferdinand.* Wait a little, my dear marshal; the intelligence contained in that
letter appears to be agreeable—the finder must have his reward."

Common as it is to jest over Kalb as if a caricature,
he could scarcely have been drawn with a more masterly
hand than the poet has displayed in the few scenes in
which he mingles; and it was scarcely possible to portray more faithfully the utter pitifulness and worthlessness of that class of men who used so readily to gather
around princes of moderate capacity and despotic nature.
Any one acquainted with such circles, will readily recall
instances of this kind of character. Upon an insig-
nificant man of this sort the demands of court society,
the habit of clothing what is common with grace, and of
giving it expression as if having weight, the handling of
what is really important with neglect and with a reckless
levity, must exert the most baleful influence; the product we see in the marshal, the moth who flits thought-

lessly in the sun of courtly favor, whereas, in Ferdinand, a character is portrayed which passion first awakes to perfect love. His father himself wonders at him, and breaks out:

"Where in the world couldst thou collect such notions, boy?"

In their disregard of consequences, father and son are alike, with this difference, that, as so often occurs, out of horror at the intriguing character of the former, the son preserves the highest purity and honor, and secures thereby an interest at once, which, in noble natures, often deepens into enthusiastic sympathy.

Even the greatest natures cannot wholly tear themselves away from the prevailing tendencies of their times ; and if Schiller fell into the manner only too common in that period of "storm and stress," and painted people the darker the higher they stood in the social scale, there is this to be pleaded in his behalf, that Wurtemberg was not lacking in originals for a style à la Höllenbreughel. It is peculiar, however, that the recognition of a rascal, par necessité, in every minister, seldom led Schiller to attack the person of the reigning prince. He contented himself with merely giving a few side-thrusts, while a modern, of equally fiery spirit, would surely have struck directly at the serenissimos.

10

A. v. Ramberg del.   C. Geyer sculp.

Louisa Miller

LOUISA MILLER.

(Love and Intrigue.)

" LOVE AND INTRIGUE," this youthful effort of Schiller, is not perfectly intelligible if the reader does not make real to himself the soil on which it grew, Wurtemberg, under the rule of Duke Charles, where Schiller received the first harsh impressions which he sought afterward to embody artistically in this play. He paints the demoralizing sway of mistresses to which this despotic, but richly endowed, and subsequently highly meritorious, prince was subject in his youth. He felt himself compelled to pass his judgment with that unsparing severity which must have been experienced by a pure, enthusiastic spirit, in view of a state of morality that met him everywhere ; he even speaks with a degree of coarseness which can only be explained on the score of the untrammelled loyalty to Nature which Schiller felt, and, in a degree, of his Shakespearian recollections.

Strikingly indicative of that epoch, is the immense chasm which separates the rank of Ferdinand from that of the musician's daughter, a consciousness of which is so incessantly appearing in the *dramatis personæ* as to make it seem almost exaggerated, whereas it is unquestionably a perfect transcript of the time.

According to the expression of Lady Milford, whose sight has manifestly been sharpened by jealousy, Louisa is "very interesting, and yet no beauty;" the artist has caught her at the moment when Ferdinand says to her :

"The drink is bad, like thy soul."

If Louisa's language seems too choice and sententious for a girl of sixteen, we must keep the fact in view that Ferdinand has sought to cultivate her intellect, has lent her books that unquestionably represented the transcendental literature of that age, and that, as an all-pervading and overmastering passion makes a poet out of every man, and gives emphasis to his language, it does so much more signally with an enthusiastic maiden.

Brought up in the peaceful stillness of her home-circle, her passion for a man higher in rank than herself suddenly takes exclusive possession of a soul hitherto given to love of God and her parents; she forgets that there are other men besides—she almost forgets that there is a God besides him who fills her whole soul; she has no longer eyes for the world, and yet she has never found it so fair; she no longer knows aught of God, and yet never before loved Him so dearly. If this excess of feeling comes to a painful issue, it is, notwithstanding, more genuinely tragic that it is not hatred, but love,

which brings her to her destruction; and all the more
tragic the stronger she grows, when her father, Wurm,
and Ferdinand himself, ascribe all their misfortunes to
her. The rude language employed by the latter against
his betrothed, when he believes her guilty, could not
possibly have come from Schiller, had it not been for
that Suabian training which clung to him so persistently.
With all their cleverness in other things, the Suabians
are to-day certainly the least chivalrous of Germans,
and the social position of their women the lowest;
although not only the beauty, but the spirit and the
natural advantages of the Suabian women, in no wise
deserve this setting aside. This Louisa shows, too, to
whose keenness, grounded in her woman's nature, and
sharpened by love, we have to ascribe the victory which
she clearly gains over the cultivated Lady Milford,
notwithstanding all her superiority of position, and her
refined dialectics. In this struggle, Louisa's power lies
in the greatness, strength, and depth of her feeling, and
the vigorous language in which she gives it expression.
The voice of the heart, in a moment of intense passion, is
as superior to the eloquence of the understanding as the
natural simplicity of popular poesy is to artistic and
elaborate verse.

But we are not able to ascribe all of this philosophic
tone of mind, all this studied casuistry, to the girl of
sixteen; it is the subjectivity of the poet himself which
here and there breaks out, and overmasters the language

employed by the characters themselves; it is the student
of the Stuttgart School, who at times reasons in so lofty
and deep a strain.

On this very account, because he portrays a part of
his personality, he succeeds admirably in representing
the unbridled foaming passion of Ferdinand, while,
though pathetic and wrought up to the highest pitch as
he was, he yet scarcely had any ear for the *naïve* beauty
of speech in a girl of humble birth, as Goethe has
painted it so wonderfully in Gretchen.

Difficult as it is to believe that Louisa spoke in words
such as Schiller has put into her mouth, the great
power of the poet is abundantly testified in her actions.
He has portrayed with wonderful accuracy the gentle,
womanly nature, more given to forbearance and self-
denial than to struggle; and everywhere subjecting itself
to duty, law, and resignation, even when her heart is
breaking, since she feels that these qualities are yet the
protection of her sex from the passion and rude egoism
of men.

That Louisa does not fulfil her oath, a compulsory
one as it was, would perhaps not be deemed correct in a
maiden of our time, when, even in the lowest classes, the
thought of revolt against divine and human laws is not
uncommon, and when it would obviously recur to the
mind of a grief-stricken girl; but, at that time, the
world was not as far advanced in ideas, and the thought
of suicide was the more obvious one. In like manner, a

comparison of the present time with that portrayed in
this play, brings us to the conclusion that the relation of
the family, as well as that to God and the state, was
much closer than at present ; and that a father was
invested with a much greater degree of power than he
possesses now.

The strength of the poetry becomes irresistible in the
last scenes, when Louisa experiences a presentiment of
death, as she sees Ferdinand, and passes her correct
judgment upon him :

"Rather than confess his own rashness, he accuses the wisdom of Heaven."

The utter devotion of woman's love, which rises
above every thought of self, appears when she learns
from his own lips the crime that he has committed
against her, and her first thought is :

"O God, forgive him! God of mercy, lay not this crime on him!"

Would this have been the first thought of a man, whom,
on suspicions equally lightly founded with this, his
betrothed had brought to the very gates of death ?

A. v. Ramberg del.   A Rordorf sculp

LADY MILFORD.

(*Love and Intrigue*)

the characters of "Love and Intrigue," owing to
exaggeration, impose upon the artist a difficult
task of Lady Milford, to whom
.... satisfactory
.... seems a
.... woman has
.... and given us the
.... g woman, whom we can, at all
events, credit with a passionate turn of thought, and
who may be easily conceived as saying:

"Woman has but to choose between ruling and serving, but the utmost joy
of power is a worthless possession, if the mightier joy of being slave of the man
we love be denied us."

A finely-organized, gifted, high-strung woman, used to
the world, equally open to good and evil influences, she
is presented in the engraving in the act of pushing away

LADY MILFORD.

(*Love and Intrigue.*)

IF the characters of "Love and Intrigue," owing to their exaggeration, impose upon the artist a difficult task, this is preëminently true of Lady Milford, to whom it is extremely difficult to ascribe any one satisfactory, leading impulse, and who, at the first glance, seems a being monstrous and impossible. The draughtsman has sought to overcome this difficulty, and given us the picture of a charming woman, whom we can, at all events, credit with a passionate turn of thought, and who may be easily conceived as saying :

> "Woman has but to choose between ruling and serving, but the utmost joy of power is a worthless possession, if the mightier joy of being slave to the man we love be denied us."

A finely-organized, gifted, high-strung woman, used to the world, equally open to good and bad influences, she is presented in the engraving in the act of pushing away the duke's present, terrified at the dreadful picture which the bearer displayed to her. If we credit the apology with which, in the exercise of wonderful tact, she

11

addresses the inexperienced major, whose feelings are
quickly touched, and who leaps readily from the deepest
suspicion to admiration and respect—if we accept that
apology, her misfortune and beauty have brought her into
a position of need from which his help alone can save her.
At bottom, she is a mere actress—affected, sentimental,
she deceives herself in dreaming that she can wash away
by a petty philanthropy the great blot of her existence,
and lightly steps over the dark spot in her history, which
could only be excused on the ground of her real love
and faithfulness for the duke. That her sense of honor
demands this, she has, in the true manner of mistresses,
no suspicion when she says to Ferdinand :

"My passions, Walter, overcome my tenderness for you."

Proud, ambitious, and, at least, open to a great degree
of passionate emotion, she is, nevertheless, too much a
courtezan to cherish any true feeling long. In her character an English element may be seen most distinctly, in
the haughtiness which she displays under all circumstances. It is betrayed, too, in that bitter spleen in
which, after her project in reference to Ferdinand had
failed, and she stood in her shame before Louisa, she
treads her whole destiny under foot, and leaves the stage
over which she had walked with victorious step ; and in
the stubborn humor, in which she imagines that she can
love a man with whom, till then, she had never spoken.
This arbitrary fantasy, which impels her to throw her-

self into the arms of one unknown to her—which permits
her to indulge the hope that a man of honor will forget
her previous career—would conceal from us the slender
consistency of her caprice, if such women did not often,
in their very caprice, betray an iron stubbornness. If
the reader will take the trouble to look at the character
somewhat closely from this point of view, to untwist the
tortuous dialectics which the poet puts in her mouth,
and in which he communicates much more what he
thinks about the character than what the character
itself thinks, he will, in spite of the meagreness of the
elaboration, be amazed at the masterly qualities brought
to view, which, with all the confusion of ideas that
marks Schiller's works in this first period, fill us at
once with astonishment and dismay. If one would know
Lady Milford as Schiller pictured her to himself, and not
as she is really represented, he must view her in the
scene with Louisa, where the proud, egotistical, fascinating nature, with more than a touch of the serpent
in it, and having remarkable alertness in turning, comes
to view; and where she pronounces her own verdict,
when she says to Louisa:

"No evasion, miss. Were it not that you depend upon personal attractions,
what in the world could induce you to reject a situation—the only one where you
can acquire polish of manners, and divest yourself of your plebeian prejudices?"

And when, later, she flares up with these words:

"I cannot be blessed with him, neither shalt thou. Know, wretched girl, that
to blast the happiness of others is itself a happiness."

Or when, in genuine English fashion, she wants to buy
of Louisa the man of her heart :

"Where am I? What have I done? What sentiments have I betrayed? To
whom have I betrayed them? Oh, Louisa, noble, great, divine soul! forget the
ravings of a maniac. ˉ Name thy wishes. Ask what thou wilt; I will serve thee
with all my power. I will be thy friend—thy sister. Thou art poor, look [*taking
off her brilliants*], I will sell these jewels, sell my wardrobe, my horses and carriages;
all shall be thine. Grant me but Ferdinand."

This not succeeding, she comforts herself at last with
the thought of the éclat which her decision to leave
the court would produce, and says :

"How the illustrious puppet will stare! The idea is singular enough, I own
—the presuming to astonish his serene numskull. Into what confusion will his
court be thrown! The whole country will be in a ferment."

While she speaks in these dozen voices within a
quarter of an hour, and shows these many sides of her
character, all of which have nothing abiding, she
justifies us in the expectation that, in order to astonish
the court, and the "illustrious puppet" still more, if she
goes away to-day she will return to-morrow.

PHILIP II.

(Don Carlos.)

GERMAN poetry has no work in which the nature of
absolute power, its inevitable effect upon the immediate
surroundings of the ruler, as well as upon every thing
that he touches, is portrayed with any approach to the
skill displayed in " Don Carlos." The chief characteristic of despotism is the repression of all true pro-
ductivity, because to produce requires a progress which
absolutism denies, and must deny — production being
the developing of an organic creation according to its
own inner laws, and therefore opposed to all external
compulsion. Despotism, in whatever form it appears,
whether as monarchical, democratic, or ecclesiastical
absolutism, has always been the sworn foe of all pro-
ductivity—has always exhibited a desire to depreciate
every thing which has vitality, and to convert its life
into a mere mechanism.

It is this element which Schiller has introduced
to us as characterizing the court and national life of
Madrid; and by it he easily succeeds in filling us with

that terror and hatred of tyranny, the excitement of
which must certainly have been one purpose of the play.
In becoming conscious of an influence so hostile to
culture, we are naturally inclined to hate the causer of
it, and all the more when his overmastering disregard of
justice becomes apparent to us. The father has robbed
the son of the lady whom he loved; the most sacred
claim of him who stands in the state second only to the
tyrant, has no weight; law exists for one man alone; for
all others there is no such word. Side by side with the
oppressed son, we see the instruments of tyranny. Since
the pleasure of free action is denied to them, they know
only one interest—their own; priests, generals, dig-
nitaries of every kind, even women, know only this
goal; and the most reckless egoism lurks everywhere
beneath the cold, polished, soulless form of courtly
manners and courtly speech; that no one expresses
himself otherwise, or apparently thinks and feels otherwise than is officially prescribed, shows us most distinctly
the weight of the burden that rests upon all. It is not
enough that the gentle Mondecar rejoices when promised
an auto-da-fé—". 'Tis only heretics they burn." even the
frivolous Eboli shrinks from the thought that she could
be considered a poorer Christian than the Marchioness
Mondecar. These two features show us admirably
where we are. The complete perversion of natural
feeling is the best preparation for the appearance of
him who is to be the representative of absolutism. His

first expression touches upon the sustaining of external
rank, whose external rigidness is well known to go hand
in hand with its internal corruption. The dispropor-
tionate severity with which Philip punishes a light
deviation from etiquette, the scorn with which he
accompanies the punishment, show us at once the coldness, stiffness, excessive jealousy, and, at length, the
cruelty of his character. Still Philip is none the less
every inch a king; one feels him to be a man born to
command, even what is common he does with a certain
dignity; majesty, and the habit of bearing rule, do not
desert him for an instant; but he shows himself as well
the pedantic supporter of a system which, at last,
presses with its leaden weight as heavily upon him as
upon others. With all his jealousy and selfishness, he
yet remains, in bearing, a gentleman; and, in him,
Schiller portrays with inimitable skill the difference
between mere external politeness and inward nobleness;
the latter quality Philip never reaches, although he never
becomes trivial and commonplace.

Philip's unfruitful greatness is thoroughly unequal
to any positive forth-putting of good; he can merely
destroy by his despotic instinct, which disregards all
personal rights, even those of his son, whom he thus
reproaches:

> "I scarce can love
> Those sons who choose more wisely than their fathers."

Philip's absolutism, however, is not an inheritance

which he is merely to receive and preserve; it lies, on
the contrary, merely in his dark and cruel nature, for
whose satisfaction he has wrought out this system of
blood. He is a tiger throughout; and his only magnanimity is that of the lion. All forbearance appears to
him to be weakness, and he is inexhaustible in schemes
involving barbaric rigidness. The evil conscience, which
no sophistry will silence, the feeling of horror at the
intermingling of sensuality and cruelty in his own nature,
is the source of a suspicion which spares no one; and
tortures those the most who stand the nearest to the
king. Even to Don Carlos he says :

> " Trust my best army to thy thirst for rule,
> And put a dagger in my murderer's hand ! "

The Machiavellism so necessary to the despot is just as
clearly shown in his words to Alva—

> " I'm pleased that Carlos hates my counsellors,
> But I'm disturbed that he despises them !"—

as the hatred that breaks out against freedom everywhere, wherever it may appear. In this respect, one of
the finest touches of the play is that he cannot bear the
Marquis Posa free. Even after the king has begun to
love him :

> " This pride I will not bear. From this day forth
> I hold you in my service. No remonstrance—
> For I will have it so."

It is the punishment of all despots that, sooner or
later, they necessarily come to see that love blooms only

in the sunlight of freedom; and that they who do not allow liberty to be known in their domain never partake, or deserve to partake, of human love; the feeling of isolation must necessarily turn their own unreciprocated affection into boundless hate, and make them malicious and cruel to the very objects of their previous kindly feeling. This is the tragic fate to which we see Philip at last succumb, whose betrayed love to Posa, who gives him up as soon as he sees his nature, is transformed into fearful vengeance against humanity, whose interests Posa preferred to the affection of the king.

The artist has portrayed, in his picture of the proud monarch, Philip's barren, bigoted, and knavish nature, joining it, nevertheless, with an unquestioned air of high breeding. As his foundation, he has taken Titian's celebrated and almost unsurpassed portrait, whose matchless power is at once a testimony of the character of the king, a judgment which, to all eternity, shall be irrefutable and irrecoverable.

12

A. v. Ramberg del.   M. Lämmel sculp.

ELISABETH OF VALOIS.

(*Don Carlos.*)

COMPULSION unnerves and disheartens weak natures, while noble and strong souls are roused by it to resistance; they love all the more purely and glowingly the freedom that is denied them.

This is taught us preeminently by the majestic character of Elisabeth, to whom the poet has imparted a profusion of admirable traits, and a reality which, in the earlier plays, we have only seen in the remarkably life-like character of the musician's wife in "Love and Intrigue." Here he has given us a figure full of dignity, greatness of soul, and truthfulness to nature; has displayed the maturity of his own power, the larger experience of life, and the closer knowledge of the human heart, which he had at this time gained through his intimacy with Charlotte von Kalb—the object of his love at that time.

The opening scene in Aranjuez displays to us, with unsurpassed skill, the painful situation of the royal lady, as well as the security with which she bears herself, and which forms so prominent a feature of her character. The high-born daughter of sunny France, trained under the humane ideas of the enlightened patron of arts, science, and all generous culture, Francis I., she can never reconcile herself to the leaden atmosphere of the gloomy, bigoted, and pedantic gravity of the court at Madrid, and longs to fly from the iron yoke of etiquette to the free air of her childhood's home. While selfish natures wish to gain freedom merely for themselves, loftier souls desire to gain it, and keep it, for others. That Elisabeth belongs to these, we see at once from the manner in which she speaks of the marriage which was to be forced upon the Eboli :

> " The man whom I reward
> With my sweet Eboli must be a man
> Of noble stamp indeed. . . .
> But we fain would know
> If he can love, and win return of love. . . .
> 'Tis a hard fortune to be sacrificed."

Her mode of thinking is more clearly manifested still, where she receives Marquis Posa, and wishes him happiness in the life he means to lead :

> " A greater prince in your retired domain
> Than is King Philip on his throne—a freer "—

or when she says to him subsequently—

> " How will my heart rejoice should this become
> A refuge for the liberties of Europe ! "

The royalness, the tone of command in her nature,

dignifies every word that she says—betrays itself not
only in the massiveness and dignity which everywhere
are hers, in the appreciation which she shows for all
great interests, but preëminently in the readiness with
which she subordinates her own personal wishes, and
even the most secret longings of her heart. It is with
some verisimilitude that Posa can say of her to the
jealous Philip :

> " She sees with some resentment her high hopes
> All disappointed, and herself shut out
> From share of empire. Your son's youthful ardor
> Offers itself to her far-reaching views—
> Her heart! I doubt if she can love."

Her feeling toward the *infante* is rather sympathy
than love; she takes an interest in him because she sees
him suffer, not because he inspires her with admiration
or reverence. These qualities she has in marked degree
for Posa. With him alone she feels that she is perfectly
understood and appreciated; she looks up to him—down
to Carlos; and when she says to the marquis about her
relation to the prince—

> " Your friend,
> Marquis! so wholly occupied your mind,
> That for his cause you quite forgot my own "—

the confession would relate much more closely to Posa
than to Carlos, as appears still more plainly from his
answer :

> " Yes, in all other women—but in one,
> One only, 'tis not so; for you I swear it. . . .

>   Then promise, queen,
> That you will ever love him. . . .
> That you will love him still unchanged forever,
> Say—do you promise?
>   *" Queen.*   That my heart alone
> Shall ever vindicate my love I promise "—

and continues—

> " You are then going, marquis, and have not
> Told me how soon, and when, we meet again?
>   *" Marquis [his face turned away].*
>   Yes, we shall surely meet again.
>   *" Queen.*   Now, Posa,
> I understand you. Why have you done this?
>   *" Marquis.* Carlos, or I myself!
>   *' Queen.*   No, no; you rush
> Headlong into a deep you deem sublime,
> Do not deceive yourself. I know you well;
> Long have you thirsted for it. . . .
>   'Tis the love
> Of admiration which has won your heart—
> Is there no hope of preservation?
>   *" Marquis.*   None. . . .
>   *" Queen [turning away, and covering her face].*
> Go! never more shall I respect a man.
>   *" Marquis [casts himself on his knees before her*
>   *in evident emotion].*
> O queen! O Heaven! How lovely still is life! "

By the side of this scarcely-veiled passionate attachment, how cool is her tone to Carlos in the last scene!—

> " We must not now unnerve each other thus.
>   . . . With his dear life
> He purchased thine, and shall this precious blood

Flow for a mere delusion of the brain?
.O Carlos, I have pledged myself for thee!
On that assurance did he flee from .hence
More satisfied."

Even the confession of attachment which she makes
to him, appears to be rather a means of quieting him
than the fulfilling of the request which the deceased
Posa left; and does not, as in the case of the latter, rise
to a devotion so entire that it would retain its object at
any cost, for she sends Carlos away; the clearest proof
that she has a larger, more richly-endowed nature, more
genuine capacity to rule, than he.

important respects inly
cinal—an amiable high

DON CARLOS.

CARLOS's nature must necessarily be formed upon Philip's system of education; for among the most destructive influences of despotism, in whatever form it appear, is this—that its iron pressure annihilates every independent growth, and that the character, prematurely compelled to assume a prescribed form, is able to attain to no free development. And so we find it in Schiller's Carlos—who, in many not unimportant respects, may differ from the · historic original — an amiable, high-spirited, fine-toned, captivating, stubborn, and capricious noble, but weak man, equally unskilled in doing, and in commanding men; now reserved and distrustful, the next moment improvident and stormy; but, above every thing, impracticable, unproductive, and apathetic; for, since no free scope is granted to him, he soon loses all relish for activity.

The first need of man—the most powerful medicament for all ills of mind and of body—is labor. The

13

struggle with a great, self-imposed task brings one to a
consciousness of his power.   This specific is, however,
denied to the future heir of two worlds after his return
from the university; and, with its lack, begins the perplexity of his spirit.   Because no healthful tasks are
prescribed to him, his whole power is directed in
the form of a sickly passion to the most unnatural
ends, and his will becomes caprice; for by no other
word can we call Carlos's love for his mother,
whom he had never yet more than half-known.
Elisabeth herself says, with entire correctness, of this
passion :

> " It is but spleen and waywardness and pride
>   Attract you thus so madly to your mother."

At bottom, it springs merely from unconscious
hostility to the tyrant who troubles his whole existence,
and whose claims, as a father, are to him a mere
abstraction, and have no power over his soul.   Let us
take his own words:

> " Am I to blame if slavish nurture crushed
>   Love's tender germ within my youthful heart ?
>   Six years I'd numbered ere the fearful man,
>   They told me was my father, met mine eyes
>   One morning—'twas when, with a stroke, I saw him
>   Sign four death-warrants.   After that I ne'er
>   Beheld him, save when, for some childish fault,
>   I was brought out for chastisement."

Where shall the love come from which, like every

other good thing, must be struggled for, won, deserved ?
Next to active labor, the need of love is the most
powerful factor in the human heart. We love in others
not that which we have, but what we lack. The poor
Carlos is deficient in strength of mind and freedom,
both of which he presupposes in the queen, and finds in
Posa; it is these that so strongly bind his weaker nature
to theirs. He, himself, confesses this cause of his affection, when he reminds his newly-found friend of the time
of youth when—

> "I had no sorrow but to see myself
> Eclipsed by thy bright genius; so I vowed,
> Since I might never cope with thee in power,
> That I would love thee with excess of love."

Noble as this sensibility is, it yet indicates, if we
must honestly confess it, a weakly nature. Manly
spirits are naturally attracted to what is general,
to ideas and things; womanly ones to what is
individual to persons. Carlos loves freedom so long
as Posa speaks to him of it; but when one fails
to stand by his side, and support him, he sinks
back into the position which he paints with the
words :

> "I, too, have had my visions of a Carlos
> Whose cheek would fire at Freedom's glorious name;
> But he, alas! has long been in his grave.
> He thou seest here no longer is that Carlos
> Who took his leave of thee in Alcala;
> Who, in the fervor of a youthful heart,

> Resolved at some no. distant time to wake
> The golden age in Spain. Oh! the conceit,
> Though but a child's, was yet divinely fair.
> Those dreams are past."

If he regards the most noble goal which he can propose to himself as a mere dream, as soon as his best prop falls, he shows his womanly weakness no less plainly when, subsequently, he finds Posa again, and cries—

> "Thus arm in arm with thee I dare defy
> The universal world into the lists"—

which certainly is no manly sentiment, since a real man, more especially if one of power, would have proposed this task to himself at all events, as Posa really does. Weak men have almost always mistrust and doubt, not only regarding others, but themselves as well; and this we see in Carlos, in the scene where the artist has represented him, in which, after Lerma's revelations respecting Posa's deeds, the prince believes himself betrayed by the latter, and breaks out—

> "I've lost him now, and I am destitute"—

and he passes true judgment upon Posa's character when he says—

> "Must not his country dearer to him prove
> Than Carlos?"

To comprehend, and possess magnanimity, are certainly very different things.

The incompleteness of his nature is no less clearly painted in his relation to the queen and the Eboli. For a man, love is no goal of life; he never gives it the first place—it has that only in the woman. A true man would not have caused the fair Eboli to sigh in vain; he would scarcely have loved the great ambitious queen, but would have contented himself with honoring her; in doing as Don Carlos does, there is something boyish.

The prince reaches the culminating point of a milk-sop, as Heine might say, when, after refusing the fair demands of the Eboli, he yet wishes to make use of her as a third party. This is a genuine German touch, and indeed there is nothing Southern in the character—a real German coloring is seen in his whole mode of thought. While Philip, Alva, Domingo, Posa, display more or less of the national character, in Carlos the Flemish-German element prevails—the blond; and, on this account, the artist has been compelled to represent him so, necessarily deviating from the authentic portraits of the historic Carlos, in which there is more of a knavish, crafty look, than could be allowed in our engraving.

Powerful shocks may drive weak men to great resolutions, but they cannot give the power to carry them into act; and if, through Roderigo's death, we see Carlos driven to a comprehension of his true duty, as is expressed in his words to Elisabeth:

"There is a higher, a more needful good
Than your possession. A brief night
Has winged the idle current of my years,
And brought me to an early ripeness"—

this immense change in his nature necessarily leads
to his destruction, the tragic element lying just in this
—that, to do his life-work, not the will is wanting,
but the power.

Fr. Pecht del.

A. Schultheiss sculp.

Marquis Posa.

MARQUIS POSA.

(*Don Carlos.*)

Low natures have no ideal goals, common ones
follow them only in youth; but noble ones retain them
till manhood, only with more earnest and steady aim.
Among the last Schiller's Posa belongs, in whom the
artist has been able to portray, with masterly skill, that
genuine greatness of soul whose sacred fire burned in
his own breast.

If, in Don Carlos, the womanly element of character is most prominent, in Posa it is the manly one
that most appears. Philip, Carlos, chief of all, the
queen, everywhere feel, in spite of their exceedingly
varied points of view, that, in him, great ideal interests
far outweigh all personal ties. That no friend, however
dear, is, with him, to be compared with the claims of
humanity, is pictured in the interview with Carlos,
where, without troubling himself much about the
prince's grief, he speaks chiefly of his undeception in
not finding him as he hoped:

"Not thus I looked to find Don Philip's son.
.... No more I see
The youth of lion-heart to whom I come
The envoy of a brave and suffering people,
But as the deputy of all mankind.
I clasp thee thus—'tis Flanders that clings here,
Around thy neck, appealing with my tears
To thee for succor in her bitter need."

It is clear that this is the scene in which the artist should represent him; where the heroism, energy, and decisiveness of his character form the most wholesome contrast to the noble but weakly nature of Carlos.

Nevertheless, Posa, although a powerful thinker, a brilliant speaker, a bold soldier, is no statesman; and it does not appear to have been the poet's intention to have drawn him as one. For this *rôle* he has too marked a preference; for the most desperate measures, too much enthusiasm; and, in all that he does, he is too easily led away by the impulse of the moment. He is the prophet of a new age—not a man of affairs. His very effort to win Carlos over to espouse the cause of the provinces, while he knew his weakness, and the fruitlessness of the effort in case of success, does not speak in his behalf; still less the announcement of his plan during the interview with Philip—brilliant as it is as a masterpiece of eloquence. No statesman would surely undertake to convert a despot of sixty years—only an enthusiast would do this; and Philip, therefore, rightly regards him as such, although he learns to love the man.

Lacking, therefore, as Posa is in balance and wholeness of character, he is yet a man of splendid endowments, displaying remarkable depth of thought in every thing that he says. An instance may be found in the manner in which he justifies himself in his soliloquy before meeting the king: ·

> "How came I here? Is it caprice or chance
> That shows me now my image in this mirror?
>   . . . . Was this but chance?
> Perhaps 'twas something more. What else is chance
> But the rude stone which from the sculptor's hand
> Receives its life? Chance comes from Providence.
> What the king wants of me but little matters—
> I know the business I shall have with him.
> Were but one spark of truth with boldness flung
> Into the despot's soul, how fruitful 'twere
> In the kind hand of Providence!"

Satisfied as we may be with this preliminary theorizing, we must be less so with the application which he makes of it—displaying the dreamer as it does. Despots may be scorched by the sparks of truth, but they are not melted by them.

If the action of the marquis does not appear to be always justified, there is no lack of power in the poet's effort to make clear to us the influence of his brilliant, earnest eloquence. There is a sustained enthusiasm, a subdued glow of sensibility, a loftiness of thought, whose magic power never escapes us, making clear to us that Philip, hard - pressed, and most sorely

14

wounded by jealousy and suspicion, must give his confidence to a man who holds such views, and must
confess—

> "Poison itself
> May, in a worthy nature, be transformed
> To some benignant use. . . .
> Ne'er met I such a man as this. . . .
> Marquis, you know mankind. Just such a man
> As you I long have wished for. You are kind,
> Cheerful, and deeply versed in human nature."

The most delicate touch is in the picture of his
relation to the queen, where she gives a sketch of him
in the words :

> "The first
> That made me feel how proud a thing it was
> To be the Queen of Spain and Spanish men "—

and he, with genuine Spanish gallantry, replies :

> "At that time I never could have dreamed
> That France should lose to us the only thing
> We envied her possessing."

It is Posa alone who gives her a glimpse into the
dark, veiled future—Posa, who offers her a ray of hope
and satisfaction ; he alone shows her that, in a manly
character, nobleness is not associated with weakness,
nor strength with cruelty. Her quiet and beautiful
confidence he reciprocates with the same, and cherishes
an enthusiasm for her which always proclaims itself in
the most tender way, whether he says to Philip—

"And there exists besides in woman's soul
A treasure, sire, beyond all outward show,
Above the reach of slander—female virtue"—

or, at the end, when he has lost his rash throw, he expresses to her, and through her to his friend, the warmest wishes of his heart:

"Here, therefore, here,
Upon this sacred altar—on the heart
Of his loved queen—I lay my last bequest,
A precious legacy—he'll find it here,
When I shall be no more. . . .
Tell him, in manhood, he must still revere
The dreams of early youth, nor ope the heart
Of Heaven's all-tender flower to canker-worms
Of boasted reason; nor be led astray,
When, by the wisdom of the dust, he hears
Enthusiasm, heavenly born, blasphemed."

Posa is a necessary victim, because, while comprehending a new epoch, he has not power enough to usher it in. He shows the way into the Promised Land; but, like most prophets, he is not able to enter in and possess it.

A. v. Ramberg del.   C. Geyer sculp.

Princess Eboli.

PRINCESS EBOLI.

(*Don Carlos.*)

IF it is the happy prerogative of the daughters of the South to commonly possess such vigorous natures that they do not need, and cannot exercise, much reflection, and, in every thing which pertains to their inner life, merely follow their instincts, they yet ordinarily use understanding and consideration for the purpose of assuring themselves of the means to gain their ends. Through this strength of will they gain that masterly *aplomb*, which is so irresistible to the man of the North, and which is so helpful to them under all circumstances. The women of the South, therefore, stand not only much closer to Nature, but they have also much more capacity than those of the North. Culture has little influence over them—it changes nothing in them, at best it lends them sharper weapons; and the compensation for culture is generally found in their native fineness of spirit, whose ready nimbleness is immensely enhanced by the rank vigor of their natures.

Such a character—its germ to be sought in a strongly-sensuous life—the poet represents to us in his Eboli, in whom he has had the skill to compensate, by a peculiarly piquant grace and sparkle, what is lacking to her in breadth of view:

> "The princess, with those merry eyes of hers,
> Has plagued me all the morning. See, she scarce
> Can hide the joy she feels to leave the country."

Thus Queen Elisabeth presents to us the charming creature who inflames the desires of the father, while she herself cherishes in her inflammable heart a hot glow for the son. That this heart of hers is not filled with enthusiasm for cockroaches and sunset tints; that she cares nothing at all about dead Nature—but only about men; that what the Germans call *Gemuth* is entirely wanting to her, is so decisive a mark of the hot-blooded Spanish woman, that only the highest gifts in Schiller could have led him to portray it correctly, without visiting the South, and seeing its fair inhabitants. It is a triumphant proof of the strength of our poet's artistic intuition. The dark-eyed daughters of Rome, as well as of Madrid, are alike in this play; their enjoyment of Nature consists in driving through the dusty *Corso* or *Prado* just as far as all the world drives, in order to see and be seen.

So far as all the world goes is the distance traversed

by the Eboli in all other things which are indifferent to
her. Scarcely is a marriage proposed to her which does
not please her, when her blood boils up, and she thrusts
the offer away; and *"convenance"* with her comes at
once to its end.

This proposition, which is to unite her to a creature
of the king, and so to the king himself, hurls into the
excited senses of the princess this one resolve—now to
lay hold herself upon him whom she really loves. Commencing the accomplishment of her plan, the hot blood
of the South, which always makes romance begin where
it ends in the North, portrays itself in her impatient
words to the page:

> " How truly blest
> Might he have been already, in the time
> You've taken to describe his wishes to me!"

The artist has pictured her with rare skill in this
situation—awaiting the object of her love. It is the
fairest inspiration—the pearl of our work! And he
does well to present her thus to us; her life knows only
two occupations—the preparing of herself for her lover,
and the gaining possession of him. Every thing else
touches her not—interests her not, or, at any rate, only
so far as it has influence upon these two leading principles. Where she loves, she grows witty, keen, rich in
thought, imposing, empty as she is in other things which
do not pertain to the chief end of her life, to which,
with reckless ardor, she sacrifices all, but for which

she desires all. How charmingly, in the celebrated *tete-a-tete*, she satirizes Carlos's grief, and, with the most graceful of summons, she knows how to answer him when she says:

> "Near such high virtue every maiden fear
> Takes wing at once. . . .
> You who in those strict courts where women rule,
> Even there find partial judges.
>   Thou gracious Heaven,
> That gav'st him all those blessings, why deny
> Him eyes to see the conquests he has made?"

Love is the only subject on which the fair princess has ever maturely thought; but when she says—

> "Love is the only treasure on the face
> Of this wide earth that knows no purchaser
> Besides itself. . . .
>   I ne'er will make
> Division of my joys. To him alone
> I choose as mine, I give up all forever.
> One only sacrifice I make, but that
> Shall be eternal"—

it is, of course, only a general theory, that readily allows of exceptions in daily fact; and, most of all, it must be confessed, in her! It is notorious that every lady, in other lands than Spain, asserts not only to her lover, but to herself as well, that she really and truly loves him— the one then favored—above all others, and that she will love him forever. A German lady, disappointed like the

Eboli in her fairest hopes, would perhaps marry out of
convenance; but give her person to a profligate, merely
out of jealousy, in order to avenge herself for a neglect
—hardly. The Eboli, on the contrary, reasons like a
genuine Spaniard, who knows nothing about renuncia-
tion; and who can say, with true pride of beauty, of
Carlos's relation to the queen:

> " Should his love prove hopeless.
> Who can believe it ! Would a hopeless love
> Persist in such a struggle ? Called to revel
> In joys for which a monarch sighs in vain ?
> A hopeless love makes no such sacrifice."

But in recklessly sacrificing every thing to love, she
does it out of revenge :

> " 'Twill cost me dear, but here my triumph lies—
> That it will cost her infinitely more "—

and Posa judges perfectly correctly, when he doubts
whether she can ever forgive being despised :

> " Love was the price,
> The understood condition of her virtue :
> You failed to pay that price—'twill therefore fall."

The instinct of women is keen, and they pass much
more accurate judgment upon one another than men do.
The Eboli feels at once, when she speaks with the queen
of Carlos, that Elisabeth does not love him ; and, from
this instant, her passion awakens for him afresh, and she
experiences the most bitter regret when she sees him

15

threatened through her mistake. But whether the touch which represents her as revering the woman who reigns in Carlos's heart, without wishing to do so, is not rather the token of a German than of a passionate Southern nature, we must leave undecided.

A.v.Ramberg del.   G.Jaquemot sculp.

A L V A .

(Don Carlos.)

ONLY a Philip can produce an Alva, because he alone can find use for one. As the master, so the servant. This accomplice of a despot is cold and cutting, not like a sword, but like an axe. As absolutism degrades the person into a thing, the duke, although not in his own view, becomes not so much the servant of the state as the mere tool of his master; nothing is so signally striking in him as the absence of all large views. Only once, in the whole play, does he rise into the higher planes of thought, where, exasperated and defamed by Carlos, he says at last, referring to his services to the king:

> "Full well he knows far easier is the task
> To make a monarch than a monarchy;
> Far easier, too, to stock the world with kings
> Than frame an empire for a king to rule.
>   . . . And how much blood,
> Your subjects' dearest blood, must flow in streams,
> Before two drops could make a king of you!"

This presupposition must necessarily lead to entirely

different conclusions, but the genuine absolutist does
not draw them.   When Carlos asks for the application,
we hear nothing further than—

> " This sword has given our laws to distant realms,
>   Has blazed before the banner of the cross,
>   And in three quarters of the globe has traced
>   Ensanguined furrows for the seed of faith.
>   God was the judge in heaven, and I on earth "—

which every hangman can say as well ; he has no other
idea than that of rude power ; he supports whatever
exists, indifferent whether it be good or bad, and therefore Carlos answers him with entire correctness :

> " God or the devil, it little matters which,
>   Yours was the chosen arm "—

and shows him thereby his place as a mere tool.   Alva
is, according to the general belief, as well as his own,
a knight and a man of honor, as he understands it,
and as, unhappily, too many others do as well ; for
his conception of honor does not hinder him from
doing all possible dishonorable deeds—listening at doors,
intriguing, becoming a pimp for his lord, intercepting
letters, becoming a general hangman, without allowing
such a dishonorable appellation to be applied to him ;
that would be a calumny which he, unquestionably,
would wash out with blood, and for which he even
takes up his sword against the son of his lord.   Here,
too, at the bottom, he is wholly in his place as a tool ;
whoever takes hold of the knife is cut.

Meanwhile, little as the duke has of higher thought and lofty motive, little else as he will be than mere arm, or right hand rather, there is one object never to be lost sight of—himself. He is conservative, and in order to sustain himself whenever he is threatened, and his place in peril, he himself becomes a revolutionist. This is seen most clearly in his interview with Domingo, where the two nobles exchange views respecting the condition of affairs. True to his part, the priest was more cunning than he, but kept his peace, thinking, "Words let slip are confidants defamed;" yet, when Alva leads off, he, too, cannot hold back with the confessions of an honest soul. The prince is the enemy of them both, that is clear; and, according to their theory, his ultimate rule will, of course, at once put throne and altar in peril:

> "He dares to *think ;*
> His brain is all on fire with wild chimeras—
> He reverences the people! And is this
> A man to be our king?"

Alva replies out of a good store of historical knowledge:

> "These thoughts will vanish when he's called to rule."

But as he none the less enters upon intrigue, he shows all the more how much more interested he is for his own sake than for that of the state. If it brings him advantage, the duke shows a surprising talent in viewing things from various sides. He is always a servant of the state, and yet he says to Philip:

> "I owe my deepest knowledge to the state,
> And my best judgment. As to what besides
> I know, think, or suspect, belongs to me alone."

True, he expresses this only to sell his secret at a higher
price:

> "Not all that stands in clear light in my eye
> Is ripe enough for the king. Will he be satisfied
> I must beg, and not, as lord, demand?"

But in such cases, as we see at once, he goes too coarsely
to work, and misses his goal. His common, low mode
of thought is clearly indicated in the first words that he
directs to Posa:

> "The king is in your hands. Employ this moment
> To your own best advantage"—

and he places the crown upon the queen's head, when,
with Domingo, believing himself to be hard pushed by
Posa, he seeks again to form alliance with Elisabeth,
whom he just before was on the point of destroying; of
course, to the welfare of the state, whose most loyal
servant he calls himself.

The face of the duke, which the artist has faithfully
copied from existing portraits of the historical Alva,
since they completely conform to Schiller's delineation,
displays, in his fixed calmness and coldness, all that
pitiless egoism which forms the foundation of his character; that view of the world is reflected in it which
recognizes mere force, and no higher quality. There is
an old age to be revered, because it makes its wearer

milder and more just, nobler and more intelligent; but this is the old age of great souls—common ones are made only colder, harder, and more egoistical thereby; their hatred, stubbornness, and intolerance increase with the burden of years; their nobler impulses, devotion, and the .smiles of joy, are the only things that the snows of age stiffen beneath its white covering; to this latter class belong the rigid features of the iron duke, upon which the curse of centuries rests; and whose portrait the poet has drawn in such wonderfully characteristic lines.

WALLENSTEIN.

(*Wallenstein.*)

WALLENSTEIN, the greatest work of our Schiller, is
also the most perfect tragedy, on the whole, which the
German theatre possesses. This has gradually come to
be a recognized fact, and, if it be so, the chief reason
lies in this, perhaps, that the hero of the mighty trilogy
is, at the same time, the figure most skilfully conceived,
most captivating, and executed, even in the smallest
details, with the most masterly touch. It is here,
perhaps, that German art has gained its only grand
success—in showing the unmistakable nature of genius,
and its almost miraculous energies.

Not as if the other characters of the play, as well as
the relation in which they stand to each other in the
advancement of the plot, are less admirable; not as if
they do not spring from the purest and highest poesy;
but they are only portrayed on single sides, while the
Friedlander is copied in every fold of his heart.

Even in the prologue, the poet transfers us to the
eminence necessary to survey the field about to be

16

described—painting to us the condition of Germany at
the beginning of the Thirty Years' War :

> " On the dark canvas of this age
> There stands portrayed a venture bold,
> And one who wears a hero's face.
> You know him well, master of hosts,
> The camp's great idol and the nation's scourge,
> The prop, and yet the terror, of his king,
> Fortune's adventurous son,
> Who, when upborne by the favor of his time,
> Honor's loftiest pinnacle quickly reached,
> And, still insatiate, soaring to loftier heights,
> Himself a victim to untamed ambition fell."

This prepares us for the play, the main theme of which
is the artistic filling out and reanimating of history :

> " Art shall now summon him before your eye,
> And cause your hearts to feel with him ;
> For Art, that binds and limits all extremes,
> Brings them all back to Nature's arms again.
> She sees man in life's earnest stress,
> And to unhappy starry influences
> Ascribes the greater moiety of his faults."

In the background are portrayed not only fearful
masses of men, but marked characters surrounding him ;
first pictured in " The Camp," and then coming before
us in " Piccolomini," they only add colossal greatness to
the figure which they introduce. Schiller has displayed
such wonderful acumen in seizing upon and illuminating
real history by the exercise of a kind of divination, he
has so remarkably anticipated the researches of later

scholars, that the artist has had little more to do than faithfully to follow the historical portraits of Wallenstein, as they have been given us by Vandyke and others.

His is a rigid, genuine soldier's face, as all the portraits give him—externally cold, yet capable of the most reckless and consuming passion; thin, with strong cheek-bones, with black, penetrating, calm, and severe. eyes. The highest power of will and action speaks from the whole head, conjoined with an impenetrable reserve —a tendency to profound meditation, and even to mystic inquiries, while a love for what is miraculous and mysterious is manifested in the immoderately high-arched forehead, and the sharply-defined sides of the head. A spirit of resolute constancy is shown by the steadfast look directed to the ground; the firmly-closed mouth, the protruding under-lip, the bold profile, the strongly-marked lower face, having something of the character of a beast of prey—the tall, compact form. Added to all this, is the stamp of the secret power of genius, not only greatness of spirit, but also that mighty power of will, which instinctively binds the masses to him, and hurries them on with him, exerting the same magical influences that the eyes of snakes effect upon birds. He is a born ruler as he is presented to us, here, in the round tower, that Thekla pictures to us, in her interview with Max and Countess Terzky, carelessly leaning upon a celestial globe, having the representations of the planets behind him, and looking thoughtfully at the tables of figures before him, where the course of the stars is represented. It is their aspect, as he makes himself believe, which drives him to action, whereas, really, it is the very supreme voice of Nature that he follows. The indestructible, rock-like faith in himself, united with that confidence in special secret forces that stand at his command—so often met in powerful natures —that connection with an immeasurable, superhuman realm, that runs through the whole play, only enhances the spell with which the hero binds us.

As the poet paints the whole course, step by step, of Wallenstein's treachery to the emperor, and suffers us to see all the motives of his heart, he does it with a skill, the like of which is nowhere to be found in German art. Accident, destiny, and necessity are here woven together in a manner which does not release our attention an instant, nor allow us to falter in our admiration of the hero whose mighty self-deception we even understand, as we see him led into error about things which commoner natures around him see completely through. He often seems to us a kind of sleep-walker, and yet we believe in his intellectual power, because we see that it springs from the same source with the inspiration of genius.

In amazement at his greatness, we almost forget to blame his boundless egoism, and the coldness with which he sacrifices every thing to the Moloch of his ambition— the only child, the wife, the youthful friend—till destiny grasps and crushes him beneath the ruins of his shattered building, just at the time when, externally blinded by the pure offering of Max, he believes vengeance removed from his own head:

> " The unpropitious gods demand their tribute.
> This, long ago, the ancient pagans knew,
> And therefore of their own accord they offered
> To themselves injuries, so to atone
> The jealousy of their divinities,
> And human sacrifices bled to Typhon.
> I, too, have sacrificed to him ; for me
> There fell the dearest friend, and through my fault
> He fell. No joy from favorable fortune
> Can overweigh the anguish of this stroke.
> The envy of my destiny is glutted ;
> Life pays for life. On his pure head the lightning
> Was drawn off, which would else have shattered me."

COUNTESS TERZKY.

(*Wallenstein.*)

I<small>F</small>, in Thekla, we see the ideal nature of woman portrayed in its fairest light, in Countess Terzky the real side of woman is pictured with perhaps greater skill. Countess Terzky is, unquestionably, one of Schiller's most perfect creations. Had she a less ambitious spirit, were she struggling for a lower goal, she had been a common *intriguante.* As the poet has represented her to us, she is not that, for, although her weapons are taken partially from the arsenal of intrigue, they are everywhere ennobled by the masterly ability with which she uses them. The charge has often been brought against women, that they make no use of intellect and understanding—that they do not summon these gifts to help them in higher tasks—but that they generally follow common ends and arbitrary caprices, using their acumen alone as their ally. Countess Terzky shows us what is unlike this, and thereby proves her greater nature. With Max she uses the small methods of intrigue, with her brother-in-law she employs a fine womanly dialectic,

but she calls them both to her aid in order to support
the world-embracing plans of Wallenstein, whose comprehensive mind finds in her a perfect echo. She is the
only woman who understands him, and approves his
schemes. Thekla is too much a woman to seek any
other satisfaction than that of her heart; she is merely
of a lofty temper, whereas Countess Terzky is her equal
in greatness of soul, and her superior in high spirit.
That, with all this, she trifles with the fortune of two
men, repels us just as in women all superiority of understanding over feeling does. But we must confess that,
from her point of view, she is right.

What to her is Max?—a good-natured, enthusiastic
young man. What Thekla—a girl just from boarding-
school—compared with the fortune of whole lands,
compared with the father's gigantic plans, compared
with him who is confessedly the highest existence that
has interest to her? To woman the ideal becomes
personal, the abstract leaves her always cold, and only
the concrete united to a person can stir her enthusiasm.
The whole soul of the ambitious, great-hearted woman
has therefore turned to the brother-in-law, who represents her ideal of a man—whose bold, comprehensive
character completely corresponds to her own, whom she
alone completely understands, and upon whom, therefore, she exercises an influence so great, since, as a
woman, she possesses much the same power of will and
knowledge of the human heart with him; and is a

statesman, almost as much as he. How skilful she is
in the art of guiding men, the poet has happily represented in the scene where she seeks to make herself
sure of Max, while promising him the possession of
Thekla :

> "Enjoy your fortune and felicity,
> Forget the world around you, meantime friendship
> Shall keep strict vigil for you—anxious, active.
> Only be manageable when that friendship
> Points you the road to full accomplishment"—

or when she says—

> "Yet I would have you look, and look again,
> Before you lay aside your arms, young friend.
> A gentle bride, as she is, is well worth it,
> That you should woo and win her with the sword"—

or when she tries to set Thekla right :

> "Did you suppose your father had laid out
> His most important life in toils of war. . . .
>   For this only
> To make a happier pair of you. . . .
>   All this methinks
> He might have purchased at a cheaper rate.
> Leave now the puny wish—the girlish feeling;
> Oh! thrust it far behind thee! Give thou proof
> Thou art the daughter of the mighty. . . .
> Not to herself the woman must belong."

Still more masterly is her dialectic with Wallenstein,
when she urges him to come, at last, to the decision to
break with the emperor. With what fineness does she

17

touch all the chords which must resound in the heart of
this man! How skilfully does she urge the sophism:

> " Planned merely, 'tis a mortal felony;
> Accomplished, an immortal undertaking;
> And with success comes pardon hand in hand,
> For all event is God's arbitrament "—

endeavoring to build a bridge for the statesman's moral
scruples, and release him from the duty of thankfulness:

> " No honest good-will was it that replaced thee—
> The law of hard necessity replaced thee,
> Which they had fain opposed, but that they could not "—

and to show him how he will remain in harmony with
himself, if he puts an end to the rebellion:

> " Therefore, duke, not thou
> Who hast still remained consistent with thyself,
> But they are in the wrong, who, fearing thee,
> Intrusted such a power in hands they feared.
> For, by the laws of spirit, in the right
> Is every individual character
> That acts in strict consistence with itself."

Countess Terzky is too much a woman, and loves
Wallenstein too deeply, to use this language if she
did not feel that it is really the deepest emotion of
her heart that she speaks out. If she is correct in
this, she reckons falsely in her belief that she can draw
Thekla into her father's plans—the same mistake that
all politicians are apt to make, when they try to lead
idealists, who are, generally, all the more stubborn,

where the politician sees no possibility of taking but one way.

Yet, if her understanding leads her astray, her heart is all the surer a guide. Her secret love to Wallenstein, which she does not herself know,. but which is the turning-point of her whole nature, and compels her to face death with him, appears everywhere in the closing scenes, and wins our whole sympathy. Who can fail to be moved when this colossal, great-minded, keen-witted woman, suspecting the tragedy that is to come, drops the words:

> " If all should fail,
> If he must go over to the Swedes
> An empty-handed fugitive, and could himself
> Endure to sink so low, I would not bear
> To see him so low sunken!"—

or when, misfortune having already broken out, she implores him not to leave her behind .

> " Leave us not in this gloomy solitude
> To brood o'er anxious thoughts; the mists of doubt
> Magnify evils to the shape of horror "—

even where her whole love becomes visible, as she seeks to nerve him up:

> " Oh! remain thou firm,
> Sustain, uphold us, for our light thou art."

How strong this passion was, is displayed best in her death-scene, where she scarcely alludes to Terzky— only speaks of Wallenstein, and completely compels

our admiration by the greatness of soul with which,
uniting her destiny with his, she speaks her dying
words:

> " We did not hold ourselves too mean to grasp
> After a monarch's crown. The crown did fate
> Deny, but not the feeling and the spirit
> That to the crown belong. We deem a
> Courageous death more worthy of our free station
> Than a dishonored life. I have taken poison!"

OCTAVIO PICCOLOMINI.

(*Wallenstein.*)

THE representation which we give of Octavio will disappoint most persons who examine this work. They will have represented the old fox to themselves as immoderately thin, dark, possibly bald; and will find themselves looking at a portly, heavy man, having, at worst, a mere snakish expression. The artist freely confesses that he formerly cherished this common idea of Octavio, deriving it, unquestionably, from the fact that he is generally represented so in the theatre. Only acquaintance with portraits of the historical Octavio, of which there are so many—some of them really admirable—has brought him to a conception of the character different from the one generally entertained. The calm coldness—the ground-feature in the character of the cosmopolitan Octavio—comports very well with perfect digestion; a thick, bloated face conceals all the better, in its soft fat, the most dangerous thoughts, the lurking look, the sharp, observing eye. Of the soldier, Octavio has only the cold-blooded, undisturbed courage while in the greatest peril ; his enemies say of him that he is better adapted to intriguing than to leading an army, which merely means that he is more a statesman than a general—has more understanding than kindling force of will ; for that he is richly endowed is shown by each one of his expressions : eloquent, courtly, polished, he chooses all his words deliberately, but tips them so sharply that, like an arrow, they strike directly at the heart of the thing or the person. While in Max there is a thoroughly true German nature, lacking not only the Italian's native love of intrigue, but, in the highest degree, opposed to it, in Octavio the keen, ultramontane spirit is unmistakable. In this view he is a worthy adversary of Wallenstein—the only one of all the generals who has loftier views, these being wanting even to Max ; they all regard war as their vocation—as the task of life which they are to undertake for itself alone, and carry cheerfully on ; he alone recognizes it as a mere means, the extremest and saddest, too, that can be appealed to, and says :

> ' There exists
> A higher than the warrior's excellence.
> In war itself, war is no ultimate purpose."

The superiority of his mind explains completely the immense influence that he exerts upon the conclusions of the other generals ; they merely bow before the power of his reasons ; he leads them according to his views, because he knows the motives which make an impres-

sion upon every one, and thus secures men to himself,
whom Wallenstein gains only by the power of his will,
and the magic of his person, to be alienated from him
afterward by the cooler and baneful superiority of his
adversary.

Octavio is too much a diplomatist, too much a man
of intellect, to have the Friedlander's genuine hero-
nature, although his thought never runs in low currents.
His prudence, his calm repose, are so strongly developed
qualities, that they dominate wherever he is; and while
one portrays him as an old fox, another as a deceitful
cat, he is never known as the crafty Italian.   Like all
gifted men without real creative power, he awakens
antagonism, and is compelled to show us, in advance,
the points in which he is superior—a thing that can be
done only by displaying his inner nature.   Wallenstein
is as little a man of real rectitude as he, follows personal
ends no less, chooses moral means no less, and only
escapes condemnation because he charms his adversaries.
Octavio's ends can as little stand before the judgment-
seat of morality as Wallenstein's.   He is no more honorable to his friend, when the latter becomes a traitor, and
his justification to Max, when the latter accuses him of
falsehood—

> " Dear son, it is not always possible
> Still to preserve that infant purity
> Which the voice teaches in our inmost heart.
> Still in alarm, forever on the watch
> Against the wiles of wicked men, e'en Virtue

Will sometimes bear away her outward robes,
Soiled in the wrestle with Iniquity.
This is the curse of every evil deed,
That, propagating still, it brings forth evil.
I do not cheat my better soul with sophisms;
I but perform my orders. The emperor
Prescribes my conduct to me.
Better far were it, doubtless, if we all
Obeyed the heart at all times; but so doing,
In this our present sojourn with bad men,
We must abandon many an honest project"—

is, after all, better grounded than the sophisms with
which Wallenstein palliates to himself his own breach
of trust. Falling away from one who is untrue to
himself is, at least, no treachery like that of the latter;
and if he appears more hateful than the one who is his
own betrayer, it is simply because the poet unsparingly
shows us the petty and dishonorable means which he
uses in order to retain the army for the emperor; while
those of Wallenstein, to lead it into revolt, are merely
hinted at—nay, even ascribed to others. It repels
us when we hear how Wallenstein, everywhere, gives
him his confidence, and even excuses him, while
we hear Octavio say that he has surrounded the
general with spies, and see how he takes Buttler and
Isolani on their weak sides. Yet the Friedlander
is certainly no more upright in his relation to the
cuirassiers, Buttler, and even Max. Octavio characterizes his relation to him best when he says to
Questenberg:

> Hypocrisy, have skulked into his graces,
> Or with the substance of smooth professions
> Nourish his all-confiding friendship. No!
> Compelled alike by prudence and that duty
> Which we all owe our country and our sovereign
> To hide my genuine feelings from him, yet
> Ne'er have I duped him with base counterfeits."

In the superstitious confidence which Wallenstein places in him, not at all rooted in his own dependence upon him, but only in his holding him to be the most skilful instrument of accomplishing his plans, there scarcely rests an obligation to become the tool as well.

Our whole sympathy is at last turned to him again, when we find this man of such marked intellectual strength approachable on one side by love and tenderness; it touches us when we see how his son's youthful purity, which he himself could not sustain in the battles of life, was so dear to him in his Max. It is one of the most poetical touches in the piece that Fate strikes the sly Octavio with its cruel scorn exactly there, where he is the most sensitive; and shows in him, no less than in Wallenstein, that one may reckon ever so skilfully, and yet the sum come out wrong at last.

Ph. Pocht del. H. Mera sculp

MAX PICCOLOMINI.

(*Wallenstein.*)

IT is a fact as striking as it is consoling, that, precisely in the times of the deepest corruption, discord, intrigue, even ceaseless bloodshed, and the horrors of all kinds which are the inseparable companions of protracted civil wars, solitary natures appear which are untouched by the general evil, and maintain an incomprehensible purity and maidenhood. Unfortunately, it is just these natures which are destined to be sacrificed, apparently fruitlessly, which struggle in vain against the current of general chaos, and, snatched away by it, perish in its waves. But their portraits, and the memory of them, are imperishable, and, just as virtue—betrayed, scorned, and despised—always gains the victory, and rises from the flames of earthly trouble purified and glistening, so do these natures, stimulating kindred souls to a noble emulation. Such have been the Christian martyrs, such uncounted heroes of faith, science, and art; such our immortal Schiller has portrayed in Max and Thekla. If, in the raging tide of reckless passions, they do perish, every noble spirit is strengthened by looking upon them, and so they fulfil the mission for which the poet has adorned them with all the charm of his genius, and crowned them with garlands, as offerings are crowned.

The first and most genuine qualities of a man, whose possession always insures our sympathy, but whose want is never forgiven, are spirit—honor. On this account Schiller portrays the youth who, in the development of the play, is to call out our sympathy above all other men, as the young hero, on whose dark locks the laurel already glitters; and Isolani says of him, " Now shall the hero be prepared." He is portrayed to us not only as brave; the first deed which is told us of him is an act of love and self-sacrifice — he delivers his father from the ranks of his enemies. Even in " The Camp," the dependence of the brave knight is shown, in the young man's being chosen as a leader, and the reputation which he enjoys with the other regiments is shown in their all choosing him to deliver their petition. They show that the true son of the camp must reflect in his own soul what beats within every genuine soldier's breast; he is the fairest type of that genuine, national soldier's spirit, whose portraiture receives its highest poetic consecration in Wallenstein. That the poet shows us how so many thousand heroic hearts choose this fiery youth as their representative, is certainly a completely correct feature of the picture; but if, thereby, he puts him in a high place, he is yet more exalted in our eyes when we see

how Wallenstein honors and loves the genuine hero-
nature in him, feels a relationship of soul to him, is borne
away, enchanted, by the stream of his pure, youthful
sensibility, which, on every occasion, breaks out full and
crystal clear.   He says of him:

> " For oh ! he stood beside me like my youth,
>   Transformed for me the real to a dream,
>   Clothing the palpable and the familiar
>   With golden exhalations of the dawn.
>   Whatever fortunes wait my future toils,
>   The beautiful is vanished, and returns not."

With a master's hand the poet displays all these
qualities at the first appearance of Max, and shows us
how, with all the enthusiasm of a youthful soul, he has
knit himself to Wallenstein.   This is portrayed, touch
by touch, in the interview with Questenberg, as only a
superior nature can do it; and yet the whole portrait
is idealized, because he only sees what finds an echo in
himself.

Yet Max has never known the charm of peace; no
conception of its quiet happiness has ever entered his
war-accustomed soul, when the view of the blessings he
enjoys is doubly enhanced by the love he experiences
for a noble woman ; now, for the first time, he experiences, with rapturous longing, that there are other good
things in the world besides the warrior's glory and the
soldier's honors.

To bind Max to himself, by such a bond, was a

master-stroke of his friend more advanced in years than
he. But when he completely succeeds, as Max himself
announces it—

> " How my heart pours out
> Its all of thanks to him! Oh! how I seem
> To utter all things in the dear name Friedland!
> While I shall live, so long will I remain
> The captive of this name "—

we are exasperated at the perfidy which must necessarily usher in the tragic end, and with the heartless
egotism with which Wallenstein himself makes his friend's
happiness an offering to his own ambition.

Thekla suspects the dreadful truth better, when, after
he has expressed his hope in her father in the words—

> " Let him
> Decide upon my fortunes. He is true;
> He wears no mask, he hates all crooked ways,
> He is so good—so noble "—

she replies:

> " That are you."

As in Thekla, so in Max, the chief characteristic
is a youthful strength of character—a fidelity to duty in
all the conflicts of life. Incomparably fine is the opposition with which he meets the dawning conviction of
Wallenstein's treachery—the acuteness with which he
conjectures all the motives that could drive him to it,
and which yet might be excusable; they find an echo in
his own pure breast, when, in the presence of his father,
he breaks out into the complaint:

> "You will, some time, with your state policy,
> Compel him to the measure. It may happen,
> Because ye are determined he is guilty,
> Guilty ye'll make him"—

Our interest in him is carried to the highest point when Wallenstein leaves no more room to doubt about his treachery, and the young man summons all the power of youthful eloquence to restrain him, moving Wallenstein, though ineffectually, for an instant.

When he sees that all is lost, that he has been alike deceived by the father and the general, an incurable break passes through his spirit, and he beautifully says:

> "Oh! woe is me! Sure I have changed my nature,
> How comes suspicion here in the free soul?
> Hope, confidence, belief are gone; for all
> Lied to me—all that I e'er loved or honored."

But only those who are like-minded can completely understand each other; and, therefore, neither Octavio, Wallenstein, nor Countess Terzky rightly judges the part that Max will take in the contest, whereas Thekla at once feels, and with assured conviction asserts:

> "His resolution will be speedily taken.
> Oh! do not doubt of that—his resolution!
> Does there remain one to be taken?"

In this last interview, which he has with Wallenstein, we see him presented after he has laid the decision in Thekla's hands, and been directed by her to his first feeling, while repelled by all others. Despair at last

seizes his heart—the thought of seeking death overcomes him ; he yields to that immoderate sensibility
which is peculiar to youth, and which never allows a
way of escape to be seen ; he devotes himself, and
the comrades who warn him of his hated duty, to
destruction :

> "You tear me from my happiness! Well, then
> I dedicate your souls to vengeance. Mark!
> For your own ruin you have chosen me;
> Who goes with me must be prepared to perish."

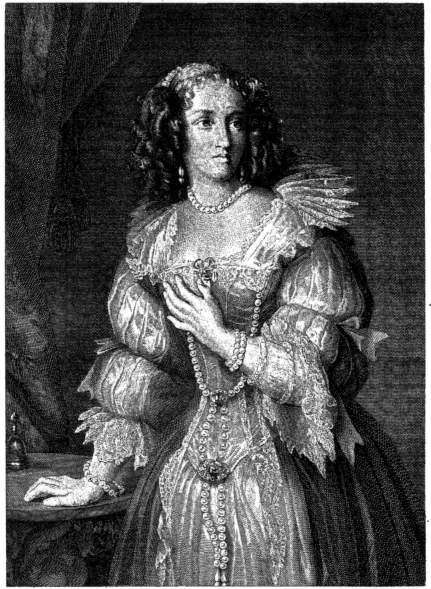

Fr Pecht del.   M. Lämmel sculp.

THEKLA.

(*Wallenstein.*)

AMONG the female characters of the great poet, perhaps no one awakens so deep feeling as that of Thekla, whom he has adorned with all the magic of his poesy, and with all the splendor of language. The blinding wealth of the latter is so great, it draws out our sympathy for this lordly figure to such an extent, that we are seldom able to take account of her special qualities. Even in that cooler age of life, when we venture not only to smile at the many illusions of youth, but, unhappily, to wonder at the enthusiasm which we once knew to be genuine, and believed to be deserved, we sometimes find Thekla's character untrue to nature, and criticise it sharply. We should, indeed, be right in this, if virtue and honor, self-sacrifice, love, and a lofty spirit were also useless illusions of youth, instead of real and lofty good things, which are able to fill our whole heart, and feed our whole life—if he were not wretchedly

19

poor, who begins to doubt their existence, and con-
sider them mere phrases.

If the poet, in his great work, imputes fault and guilt
to all, and yet lets the only innocent ones, Max and
Thekla—these pure and youthful forms—fall as the first
victims in this conflict of irreconcilable and selfish
natures, the effect is all the more tragic and painful
when we fully perceive that the necessity and inevita-
bility of their destruction are caused directly by this very
purity—this want of capacity of trifling with any moral
condition, or any dictate of honor and duty.

Thekla has just come from the convent; the poisonous breath of the world has destroyed none of her
moral convictions, she has not yet learned to accommodate herself to all changes, she is a thoroughly
complete, unbroken nature — noble, enthusiastic, high-
spirited, violent too, unbending, bold, and defiant—like
her father. Into this soul, nourished hitherto in the
quiet of the cloister, there streams, all at once, the sunlight of love, awakening her whole being into life, and
bringing her instantly to a consciousness of all her
powers.

It is an old proverb—that love makes women
wiser, but men blinder than they were before; and
so here, while Max no longer sees what is going on
around him, the inexperienced, timid maiden — suddenly made keen, strong, wise, and careful—detecting
instantly where danger threatens her lover, and who is

dealing honorably or falsely, warns Max against "these Terzkys :"

> "Don't trust them, they are false. . . .
>
> I saw at once
> They had a purpose. . . .
>
> To make us happy,
> To realize our union, trust me, love,
> They but pretend to wish it."

She feels that she cannot build at all upon her mother; she finds her father too busy:

> "Only he's so occupied,
> He has no leisure time to think about
> The happiness of us two."

How absolutely this nature surrenders itself to the entire power of love, is shown by her care for her lover:

> "Where in this place couldst thou seek for truth,
> If in my mouth thou didst not find it?"

or when she sings:

> "I have enjoyed the happiness of this world;
> I have lived, and have loved"—

or when she says:

> "Is this new life which lives in me?"

In this passion, as in every other, the egoistical element would trouble us, but Thekla's noble nature bears her over this rock, and, if she is

resolved to stake every thing on the possession of
her lover—

> "The strong will I've learned to know,
> The unconstrainable in my breast,
> And I can reckon every thing at the highest "—

she yet hallows this to our feelings by the boundless-
ness of her sacrifice, but, most of all, in that love is
more sacred than the lover—his honor is more to her
than his person, and she hesitates not an instant in
sacrificing her own happiness to his honor. That she
would rather give up him, who is a god to her, than
see a blot upon his reputation, is a feature that not
only manifests her high spirit, but a genuine womanly
character.

The final scene, in which Max confides to her delicate
feeling the decision respecting his action as well as his
honor, is not only one of the most thrilling of the
whole play, but it rests also on a deep knowledge
of the human heart; it is that genuine sensibility to
every thing noble, in the true womanly nature, to
which Max, burdened with tumultuous doubts, turns,
and implores her:

> "Lay all upon the balance—all. Then speak,
> And let thy heart decide it "—

and she replies:

> "Oh! thy own
> Hath long ago decided. Follow thou
> Thy heart's first feeling "—

and then, full of presentiment, continues :

> ' Even me
> My father's guilt drags with it to perdition."

She demeans herself, as Friedland's proud daughter,
when the evil day has broken upon her ; we see
the working of a dark hopelessness upon a spirited
soul, in her insisting upon hearing a second time
the story of the Swedish captain. It is not empty
pathos, but the dry tone of despair, which finds
no relief in tears, when she says reproachfully to
Neubrunn :

> " Had he a soft bed
> Under the hoofs of his war-horses ? "

At last she succumbs to the superhuman power of
fate. After the destruction of her lover she does not
wish to live, and gives plain expression to this when,
thinking of his faithful companions, she says :

> ' They would not
> Forsake their leader even in his death.
> They died for him, and shall I live ? "

The artist has taken her in these last scenes. In
the blond, maidenly face, with its lofty, intellectual
brow ; large, eager eyes ; small, but decided mouth,
with its full lips and its firm chin, we see the genuine
daughter of her father. His boldness and unbending will
are there, his egoism is translated into the enthusiasm

and idealism of the woman; the pride of the nature born to command, and the native nobility, speak in the grand and royal form—not only of the head, but of the figure. There is something of the hero—there is something Titanic—in this blood; this race can be crushed, but not bent.

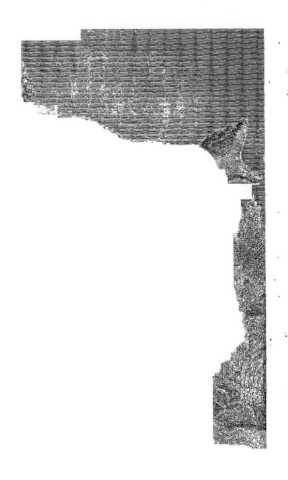

...t del.   A. Schultheiss sculp.

THE CAPUCHIN.

(*Wallenstein.*)

THERE is a rudeness which, as the daughter of a natural coarseness, as well as of straightforwardness, and a sense of honor, is harmless, and must be put up with; since what there is disagreeable in it is compensated by the fact that you, at least, know where to find the man who has it. But there is another kind, used only as a mask, to give a pretentious look to subtlety. Of the latter dangerous sort, where the serpent of a priest's cunning lurks beneath the roses of a soldier's roughness, is that found in the Capuchin, whom Schiller introduces to us, to whom, in connection with the master of the guard, he has assigned the intriguer's part in the great trilogy, and who displays to us, at the very outset, where Wallenstein's chief enemies are to be sought.

As an external profession, a channel for his secret activity, the duty is assigned him of caring for the spiritual concerns of the soldiers—of seeing that they are not wholly given over to evil. Certainly a hard task, and one that better men than he might fear, when

having to deal with such desperate patients, who say,
as Holk's *Jager* says :

> "Idle and heedless I'll take my way,
>   Hunting for novelty every day."

Further on we see the idea developed, when the same
Jager says of the army :

> "One crime alone can I understand,
>   And that's to oppose the word of command.
>   What's not forbidden, to do make bold,
>   And none will ask you what creed you hold."

For comrades who hold such views, and whose ideas
of duty are so general in their application, we want, of
course, potent means, such as are given in the world-
renowned, bold dialectics of the Capuchin. These are,
perhaps, borrowed from the incomparable sermons of
Abraham a Sancta Clara. At all events, Schiller has,
unquestionably, been indebted to this immortal type of
the tone of a Capuchin for the coloring of his own.

In Schiller's friar we have, then, a philosopher of the
Cynic order—not, by any means, a spare, black-galled
fanatic, living, like the Preacher in the Wilderness, on
locusts and wild honey, but a well-fed, red-haired, big-
bellied parson, with powerful lungs and still better
digestion, lacking neither in understanding nor in wit,
least of all in a bull-dog spirit of contention, and a love
of intrigue. He has become a priest, not from a spiritual
nature, but because he is too lazy to do any thing else.

He has tried many parts in the drama of life, and learned that, according to his way of thinking, they are all worthless. In order to be a Capuchin, one must be either tolerably stupid and bigoted, or have a strong touch of humor, laziness, cynical contempt for good things, and a love of rule. Any other than such a rough and spendthrift growth would scarcely get on in the rude air of the camp.

The Provincial Father of Vienna has given him complete instructions, and he appears upon the field of operations thoroughly equipped. At the outset he makes his points well, and, in the consciousness of their merits, the soldiers take very quietly the incisive words of praise which he deals out to them with drastic eloquence. We never oppose the truth when it surprises us, and is presented with courage and strength, least of all when humor and a piquant application take off what is most offensive; and, in this play, the orator makes use of highly figurative speech for the manifest purpose of making his roughness more agreeable, and winning the regard of his hearers.

He has probably hoped that, according to the old receipt, a half-dozen sentences strung together, and confessed to be indisputable, would pave the way for a false and sophistical application, which he might induce the hearers to swallow; this stroke of policy often succeeds, particularly when a few good points are made at the end of all, and no time left for reflection.

20

So, for example, if our Capuchin begins by painting
the political condition, and says—

> "Why, folding your arms, stand ye lazily there,
> While the furies of war on the Danube now fare,
> And Bavaria's bulwark is lying full low?"—

every one knows, nevertheless, that the army is here, in
Bohemia, taking care of its belly, and "grumbling a
little;" and just as true it is that—

> "In sackcloth and ashes, while Christendom's grieving,
> No thought has the soldier his guzzle of leaving."

There is very little to be objected when he goes on, and
endeavors to discover the cause of the war, and says:

> "For sin is the magnet, on every hand,
> That draws your steel throughout the land.
> As the onion causes the tear to flow,
> So vice must ever be followed by woe"—

or, when he discourses to the soldiers:

> "But he who 'mong soldiers shall hope to see
> God's fear, or shame, or discipline, he
> From his toil, beyond doubt, will baffled return,
> Though a hundred lamps in the search he burn."

Down to this point, what he says is incontestable,
and is quietly put up with, either from a consciousness
of fault, or as the result of his wit; his words are even
calculated to produce some effect, but, unfortunately, the
orator, growing bold, in the hope of following up his
good opening with what is false, loses all hold upon his

audience, when he unmasks his battery, and begins to
deal with calumnies :

> "But how should the slaves not from duty swerve ?
> The mischief begins with the lord they serve ;
> Just like the .members, so is the head,
> I should like to know who can tell me his creed."

This evidently purposed side-thrust at once calls forth
opposition ; he seeks to do away with the effect by
increasing his strokes, as well as by using a couple of
incontestable arguments :

> "Did he not boast with ungodly tongue
> That Stralsund must needs to his grasp be wrung,
> Though to heaven itself with a chain it were strung ?"

But going on with his calumny, and using these words
about the general :

> "Denying, we know,
> Like Saint Peter, his Master and Lord below"—

which the soldiers, at least, cannot know. And when, at
last, he blurts out :

> "He calls himself rightly the stone of a wall,
> For, faith, he's a stumbling-stone to us all"—

it doesn't help him at all, and he sees upon his side only
those who have not understood his words, and merely
trust his black coat, the Croats.

The same fate strikes the angry field-preacher which
makes so many court-preachers its victim, who pursue
just the reverse course to his, making men swallow, with

entire equanimity, a pack of flattering lies, because they
taste well.   But, in the end, the lies, as well as the liar,
are cast out, as soon as the hearers understand the man,
and have begun to mix a little unpalatable truth with
the draught.   In every case we find that, to preach to
the mighty, whether it be a single man or a mass, is a
hazardous thing, if there be knavery in the preacher's
mind that untones the morality of his words.

Gustel von Blasewitz.

GUSTEL VON BLASEWITZ.

(*Wallenstein.*)

A LONG period of war, like a long peace, calls forth
peculiar characters—a class only possible under such
circumstances. Wallenstein, Max, Isolani, and many
others, cannot be comprehended, except in connection
with this wearisome contest; and just as little should we
know the two worthies, to whom the duty has fallen,
in the drama, of providing for the spiritual and the
corporeal man—the Capuchin and Gustel von Blasewitz.
These he makes play their part with so much energy,
that, in spite of the few, though bold and secure, strokes
by which they are painted, they are both impressed in
the strongest manner upon our memory. This is particularly the case with Gustel, who enjoys, therefore, a
well-grounded popularity in both hemispheres, and has
a great number of warm admirers among all recruits,
cadets, and corporals, who betake themselves to *belles-
lettres* during the numerous hours in which they are
disengaged from duty.

Schiller derived this comical name, as is well-known,

from the daughter of a tavern-keeper in Blasewitz, a village on the shore of the Elbe, near Dresden, and directly opposite Loschwitz, the place of Schiller's sojourn at that time. The girl, who was renowned for her beauty, bore the real name of Augeste Segadin. Her charms drew a great number of young and merry spirits to the charming village on the river-bank, and among them was the poet. At that time he, in connection with Korner and Naumann, was having theatrical representations. He wished to secure the assistance of Gustel in these, but she always refused. He threatened, nevertheless, to bring her upon the boards, and out of this threat sprang the name that gave our Gustel a very unwilling and unwelcome immortality. With that excessive want of humor, which characterizes many of the Saxon maidens, she never pardoned the poet to her dying day. Soon after this Schiller episode, she married a Dresden senator, Renner by name, and died as recently as 1856, a widow of ninety-four years. She was always extremely sensitive when conversation turned upon this unwelcome part that she had played; and we can readily understand that Schiller has made no use of the original, except to borrow her name.

With all the divergence of the Gustel, whom the poet has represented as so stout and strong, from the over-precise senator's wife, yet she perhaps can claim just as respectable a number of admirers, and we can hardly mistake if we conjecture that a large share of them are proud of her friendship. Even her " old acquaintance," tall Peter of Itzehoe, says :

"Why have the lords of the regiment
Lost their hearts over this pretty face?"

The epoch of her supreme brilliance is, to be sure, almost gone. The delicate little plant of former years has expanded into a more corpulent growth, and, during this incessant exposure of camp-life, has become rather weather-beaten. She is a person all the more strongly settled and self-centred, from the fact that the Scot, who had before travelled with her, had run away with every thing which she had laid up, and left her nothing but " the brat there," which the schoolmaster receives. If the Scotchman has robbed her of a good share of the material fruits gained in these campaigns, he could not, at any rate, take away all traces with himself, and " the tall Peter" answers tolerably ungallantly to her remark —that she had seen many cities, and become acquainted with many customs since " the rough broom of war had swept her from place to place"—" Yes, you show it." Meanwhile, not every necessity of love seems to have been erased from this tender heart, and the black eyes look out tolerably inquisitively into the world; only you notice that, in the genuine manner of hosts, her friendliness seems a little studied now, and put at the special service of those who drink several bottles of Melniker,

and—pay for them. In spite of her complaints and her
everlasting trouble, she has prospered well in business,
as may be seen from the fact that she is able to lend
some cavaliers—among them, "the bad payer," Isolani
—two hundred thalers, and that half the army stands in
her books. Once in a while she decks herself out to the
utmost ; beauties as much faded as hers bear much
decoration. Whether she has paid hard money to the
jeweller for her silver chains and garnets, or, in a
cheaper fashion, gained them from Holk's *Jagers* and
Croats, for cancelled bottles of Melniker, we will not
carefully inquire, but content ourselves with this, that
" if the rose adorns itself, it adorns the garden too." It
might be as little advisable, too, to make careful investigations of what goodwife of Nuremberg or Pilzen she
has " borrowed" the fur-hood with which she decks
herself while in winter - quarters—a head - dress which
hostesses seem to have taken a particular fancy to, they
being met, at the present day, through all Bavaria—from
Bohemia to Lake Constance—on the heads of well-to-do
farmers' wives and peasant-women.

Although we have such scanty hints respecting the
past life of our Gustel, yet there are enough to convince
us that her strong, sensuous nature, joined with a certain
rude grace, was what carried her into the camp rather
than any unhappy love. She does not appear to cherish
the purpose of dying of a broken heart about that
unhappy affair with the Scotchman, and, with the tact

of women· of her class, she soon devotes herself to the
education of the recruit who, as we know, "has expec-
tations," and instructs him, without delay, in dancing.
Whether she will impart to the novice any thing of the
art of war we must leave an unsettled question; but, as
she speaks of· "the best squadrons," she can, at all
events, lay claim to the possession of no inconsiderable
amount of strategy and tactics, and she appears to be at
home in the art of taking by storm.

If the poet has given us her portrait with a few
masterly touches, he was, unquestionably, assisted by
his own years of experience in the camp, where he,
doubtless, met many such characters as she, whence
he could readily borrow their language, if not their
names.

21

Elizabeth.

ELIZABETH, QUEEN OF ENGLAND.

(Mary Stuart.)

It would be interesting to know accurately the course
of thought pursued by Schiller which led him to repu-
diate his former views respecting that great queen,
to whom England is indebted for a large share of her
glory and prosperity; to know what induced the poet
to treat her with such repulsive hardness, and only
here and there to recognize the energetic nature, the
great, royal soul, the representative of the mighty principle of Protestantism; whereas Mary, who represents
Catholicism, is painted with all the intoxicating bril-
liancy of color which characterizes her faith. This
is a concession to romanticism not elsewhere met in
Schiller.

Even in the first act, where Burleigh indicates to
Paulet the necessity for Mary's death, as well as the
grounds that make the accomplishment of it perilous, we
are prejudiced against Elizabeth:

"She fears to speak her wishes, yet her looks,
Her silent looks, significantly ask—

> ' Is there not one amongst my many servants
>   To save me from this sad alternative ? ' "

While the aversion of the Protestant people to Papal rule, as well as the wish, growing out of it, for Mary's execution, are thus painted—

> " This was the country's ceaseless fear—
>   That she might die unwept by heirs,
>   And England wear again the Papal fetters,
>   If Mary Stuart followed, bearing rule "—

we can, notwithstanding, scarcely discern the love of the people for Elizabeth. And if, on the queen's first appearance, she gives true expression to the feeling of her greatness in saying of her people—

> " And I must offer up my liberty,
>   My virgin liberty, my greatest good,
>   To satisfy my people ! Thus they'd force
>   A lord and master on me ! 'Tis by this
>   I see that I am nothing but a woman
>   In their regard. And yet methought that I
>   Had governed like a man and like a king "—

yet the hardness repels us with which, directly after, she runs away from Mary's petition for mercy; as does the hypocrisy with which she meets Burleigh's plea that Mary's death is necessary, by a pretended horror at all bloodshed ; and as does the coldness with which, directly after, she takes up Shrewsbury in his defence of Mary—

> " Lord Shrewsbury is a fervent advocate
>   For mine and England's enemy. I must
>   Prefer those counsellors who wish my welfare "—

indicating clearly enough her own temper. Only once
do we see her moved — when she receives Mary's
letter; and even then there is a touch of malice in
her emotion when she sighs:

> " Oh! what is man? What is the bliss of earth?
> To what extremities is she reduced
> Who with such proud and splendid hopes began!"

But, directly afterward, she gives correct utterance to
the feeling of tragic necessity, which compels her to
destroy her adversary; and while the result comes
clearly before our eyes—

> " The blame will ever light on me—I must
> Avow it, nor can save appearances,
> That is the worst "—

she yet exasperates us to the highest degree by the
hypocrisy which she shows in trying to avoid this result,
and the baseness with which, while she seeks to urge
Mortimer on to murder the Scottish queen, she proposes
to bestow her own favor upon him as the reward of his
deed. Mortimer is entirely right when, passing judgment on this boundless egoism, he says that, being
capable of no devotion to her, he deserves none from
her to him.

After this outbreak of mortal hatred and most
repugnant wantonness, it is a relief when, in the presence
of Leicester, she again becomes a queen:

"But I am not so blest. 'Tis not my fortune
To place upon the brows of him, the dearest
Of men to me, the royal crown of England.
The Queen of Scotland was allowed to make
Her hand the token of her inclination.
She hath had every freedom, and hath drunk
E'en to the very dregs the cup of joy."

But these reflections do not hinder her from appearing, directly after, with all her womanly weakness, and
saying :

"And is it really true that she's so fair?
So often have I been obliged to hear
The praises of this wonder."

Even the lower motive, which her favorite places
before her, works upon her—

"For though you should conduct her to the block,
Yet would it less torment her, than to see
Herself extinguished by your beauty's splendor.
Thus can you murder her as she hath wished
To murder you"—

and she allows herself to be really drawn into the
toils.

In the celebrated scene that follows between the
two queens, Schiller has again caused Elizabeth to
appear in an odious light, and no less so when the
queen speaks of the impossibility of a reconciliation
between herself and the Church whose representative
Mary is :

"Your friendship is abroad,
Your house is Papacy, the monk your brother."

Here our understanding would be entirely convinced, if our feelings were not so deeply wounded at the display of needless personal hatred against the unprotected enemy at her feet.

Driven by this hate, exasperated to the utmost by the meeting with Mary, and the treachery of Leicester, she at last signs the death-warrant, but not without first ringing the changes of hypocrisy again, and also not without a presentiment that her purpose will not reach its goal:

> "Ah! how much I fear,
> If now I heed the multitude's demand,
> The time will come when I shall hear
> A voice all different! Yes, even they
> Who drive me now by force unto this deed,
> Will sternly blame me when the act is done."

In this moment of anxious doubt and sudden determination, the artist has caught Elizabeth; and we believe that he will be completely justified, if the reader confesses that he has succeeded in bringing out what is great, colossal, and really kingly in her nature.

If Elizabeth speaks of the certainty that the judgment has already been accomplished—

> "I am Queen of England!
> Now have I room upon the earth at last.
> Why do I shake? Whence comes this aguish dread?
> My fears are covered by the grave. Who dares
> To say I did it? I have tears enough
> In store to weep her fall"—

it is at least true, if not noble ; and that the hypocrisy
with which she tries to rid herself of the appearance of
the deed finds no credence, that the deed itself does
not bring her the fruit that she expects from it, since it
robs her of her lover—the woman conquered, while the
queen triumphs—this is the tragic element in the destiny
of this colossal character.

A. von Ramberg del.

L. Sichling sculp.

Mary Stuart.

MARY STUART.

THE Scottish queen is indebted to the golden magic veil of poesy which our Schiller has woven about her fascinating head, if her memorial stands before us invested with all the glory of misfortune and an heroic death. In her the poet displays the inmost character of woman more than in any other of his plays. Although, he ascribes to her the common infirmities of her sex, as well as a certain intractableness of temper, yet he increases the power of her influence over others, by investing her with wonderful fairness and attractiveness of soul, as well as of body. These qualities draw every one powerfully to her, while her fortunate rival is portrayed as the possessor of a spirit of evil, and a double-minded character, without any atoning features —a portrait which cannot be historically true.

To such a degree has the poet thrown the charm of this mild beauty over the unfortunate queen, it permeates and adorns every thing that she says and does to such an extent, that she appears to us all the more

22

seductively the ideal of a weak woman, while he denies
the faintest trace of such a gift to the more manly soul
of her adversary, and compels us thereby to take part
with him in favor of the fair unfortunate ; for who
would not rather be infatuated by the charm of sense
than led by the dry understanding ?

If his portraiture has not divided, with historical
accuracy, the light and shade between the two enemies,
at any rate, Schiller is not silent respecting Mary's guilt.
He paints it in the very outset of the play. Mary's own
nurse says of the queen's relation to Bothwell :

> " Your ear was no more open to the voice
> Of friendly warning, and your eyes were shut
> To decency ; soft female bashfulness
> Deserted you. Those cheeks, which were before
> The seat of virtuous, blushing modesty,
> Glowed with the flames of unrestrained desire."

But while he passes, with a few lines, over Mary's
double guilt, from that time, on, we see only Mary's
repentance and majesty—only the cruel tyranny that
casts her down, only the wrong that is done her—and
wonder at the courageous spirit, as she defends herself
against Burleigh.

If, in this brilliant defence, the unhappy sufferer wins
our heart, she completely captivates us in the scene
where she takes her walk in the park—a passage in
which the utmost splendor of poetry is poured over her :
and whose heart is not touched when the unfortunate

woman emerges from her damp cell, which has for
months enclosed her, and paints her hope and rapture
in the words:

> "Freedom returns. Oh! let me enjoy it!
> Let me be childish—be childish with me.
> Have I escaped from this mansion of mourning?
> Holds me no more the sad dungeon of care?
> Let me, with joy and eagerness burning,
> Drink in the free, the celestial air.
> Fast-fleeting clouds, ye meteors that fly,
> Could I but with you sail through the sky,
> Tenderly greet the dear land of my youth!"

Do we not seem to hear the very beating of her heart,
see the wringing of her hands, and the tears of the
delighted woman?

The artist could scarcely have selected a more
favorable moment for his delineation than this scene,
which leaves no eye dry, and which makes us think
entirely of the pain endured by this charming creation,
and forget all her guilt. Even when her womanly
anger flames up afresh, as she hears the approaching
steps of her tormentor—

> "And nothing lives within me at this moment
> But the fierce, burning feeling of my wrongs,
> My heart is turned to direst hate against her"—

we feel with her, as well as when it seems to her that
nothing good can come out of it, since she herself is far
removed from forgiving her adversary; and that the

whole unbent pride of the queen lives in her when
she says :

> " The voice of Heaven decides for you, my sister,
>
> Your happy brows are now with triumph crowned,
>
> I bless the power divine which thus hath raised you "—

we find just as rational as that, when the woman in
her is most deeply calumniated, she flashes up with a
glow :

> " My sins were human and the faults of youth ;
>
> Superior force misled me. . I have never
>
> Denied or sought to hide it. . . .
>
> Woe to you when, in time to come, the world
>
> Shall draw the robe of honor from your deeds,
>
> With which thy arch-hypocrisy has veiled
>
> The raging flames of lawless, secret lust !
>
> If right prevailed, you now would in the dust
>
> Before me lie, for I'm your rightful monarch."

Here the colossal power of her nature breaks forth, and
our fair queen thinks of nothing but the satisfaction at
having gained the victory in this duel of tongues :

> " Now I am happy, Hannah, and at last,
>
> After whole years of sorrow and abasement,
>
> · One moment of victorious revenge !
>
> A weight falls off my heart, a weight of mountains,
>
> I plunged the steel in my oppressor's breast."

But this triumph instantly brings the severest penalty
that could come to her. Through Mortimer, it is
shown to her that her enemy, Elizabeth, is really right,
that she occupies a place, in the eyes of a friend and
dependant, as low as in the eyes of her adversary ; and

learns of him that this supposed victory of hers has awakened nothing but the wildest sensual desires :

> "Thine is the palm, thou trodd'st her to the dust,
> Thou wast the queen, she was the malefactor,
> I am transported with thy noble courage,
> Yes, I adore thee—like a deity,
> My sense is dazzled by thy heavenly beams.
> .... How thy noble,
> Thy royal indignation shone, and cast
> A glory round thy beauty! Yes, by heavens!
> Thou art the fairest woman upon earth."

And when she says, putting him off—

> "My woe, my sufferings should be sacred to you,
> Although my royal brows are so no more"—

he has no other reply than—

> "Thou art not unfeeling,
> The world ne'er censured thee for frigid rigor;
> The fervent prayer of love can touch thy heart,
> Thou mad'st the minstrel Rizzio blest, and gavest
> Thyself a willing prey to Bothwell's arms"—

certainly the lowest humiliation that could come to her.

It is a peculiar feature of woman's character, that when the spirit to do has gone, that to bear remains. In this the weakest woman surpasses the strongest man, and even Mary finds her whole womanly purity and royal dignity again, when her every hope has vanished, and there remains no prospect except of the scaffold. From this time, on, we see only what is noble and

touching in her; whether she shares the grief of the
old knight, at the loss of his nephew, or comforts
her women, or shows, at the confessional, the clearest
insight into her faults—

> ' My heart was filled with thoughts of envious hate,
> And vengeance took possession of my bosom. . . .
> Ah! not alone through' hate—through lawless love
> Have I still more abuséd the sovereign good "—

or takes her leave of Leicester—

> "To woo two queens has been your daring aim.
> You have disdained a tender, loving heart,
> Betrayed it in the hope to win a proud one "—

she never loses her calm, resigned dignity, and just as
little her hold upon our constantly growing sympathy.

A. v. Ramberg del.   V. Froer sculp.

LEICESTER.

(Mary Stuart.)

IT is just those women who are richly endowed, and have powerful natures—this is an old experience—who commonly bestow their favor upon very unworthy men, and suffer themselves to be blinded merely by the sensuous charm of a handsome person. Thus far it is certainly a fine, psychologically correct touch, that Schiller portrays the lover of two great queens as an ignoble man; that he endows him with an overweight of pitiful weakness, such as he gives to no other character in any of his plays. This, doubtless, limits the tragical effect of Leicester's character, since horror, but certainly not disgust, belongs in the circle of emotions which tragedy should call forth.

The effect of Goethean characters—such as Clavigo, Weisslingen, and others—appears here unmistakably; but Goethe had the skill to clothe these characters with a certain seductive amiability, which grows base out of weakness, and by no means out of a conscious purpose. Lord Leicester, on the other hand, has no particle of excuse for his baseness, nor does he reconcile us to himself by his death, as do Clavigo and Weisslingen, but, by his flight by ship to Frankfort, he puts the capstone upon his baseness.

Let us endeavor to see what there is in him which can explain the tenderness of both the queens toward him.

The first thing that we learn respecting him is, that Elizabeth's favorite, and Mary's lover, pronounced, without hesitation, at the court, in favor of the death of the latter; but afterward, when Elizabeth appeared to give a favorable ear to the French propositions for an alliance, he betrayed her as well, in endeavoring to postpone the execution of the sentence. He makes here that notable, fine discrimination of his between the duties of the judge and the statesman—

> " 'Tis true I, in the court of justice, gave
> My verdict for her death. Here, in the council,
> I may consistently speak otherwise;
> Here right is not the question, but advantage "—

which, at least, speaks favorably for his acumen, his practised skill, and presence of mind. Of these qualities, he gives, at once, a further proof, when Mary begs an interview with Elizabeth, and Burleigh dissuades the latter from it. Leicester knows, instantly, how to take Elizabeth on the weak side—

> " Let us, my lords, remain within our bounds.
> The queen is wise, and doth not need our counsels
> To lead her to the most becoming choice "—

the language always addressed to princes when their
flatterers seek to drive them to a foolish act, and an
honorable man dissuades them.

What his real relation to both the queens is, he
confesses with cynic openness to Mortimer:

> "You seem surprised, sir, that my heart is turned
> So suddenly toward the captive queen.
> In truth, I never hated her. . . .
> Ambition made me all insensible
> To youth and beauty. Mary's hand I held
> Too insignificant for me. I hoped
> To be the husband of the Queen of England.
> Now, after ten lost years of tedious courtship
> And hateful self-constraint, oh, sir, my heart
> Must ease itself of this long agony. . . .
> To lose, and at the very goal, the prize!
> Another comes to rob me of the fruits
> Of my so anxious wooing. . . .
> Thus fall my hopes. I strove to seize a plank
> To bear me in this shipwreck of my fortunes,
> And my eye turned itself toward the hope
> Of former days once more."

A more amiable confession could scarcely be made, and
it is not exactly conceivable how Mortimer could go a
step farther in his confidence after it.

A deep knowledge of woman's heart is certainly not
to be denied to the smooth and courtly lord; the most
gifted woman would rather hear her skin praised than
her brain; and even Elizabeth, when she discovers him
with Mortimer, is silenced when, with quick presence of

23

mind, he pretends to be overcome by the splendor of her
beauty.   This single touch would be sufficient to clear
Schiller of the reproach of not knowing woman's
heart.

When any one undertakes to lie to any man, but,
more especially, to one of very superior mind, he ought
not to do it on a small scale, but to pile up his falsehoods to a colossal height ; the little lie is much
sooner detected than the big one.   When it is " very
steep," it is thought there must be something in it ;
one would not venture so far with an understanding
known to be powerful.   Care must be taken, in all
these cases, that the lie hinges directly upon what is
either feared or wished.   True to this prescription,
Leicester says to Elizabeth—

> "But I love *you*, and were you born of all
> The peasant-maids the poorest, I the first
> Of kings, I would descend to your condition,
> And lay my crown and sceptre at your feet. . . .
>   I placed, in thought,
> You and Mary Stuart side by side.
> Yes, I confess I oft have felt a wish,
> If it could be but secretly contrived,
> To see you placed beside the Scottish queen.
> Then would you feel, and not till then, the full
> Enjoyment of your triumph. She deserves
> To be thus humbled. She deserves to see
> With her own eyes, and envy's glances keen,
> Herself surpassed ; to feel herself o'ermatched .
> As much by thee in form and princely grace,
> As in each virtue that adorns the sex "—

which is in very striking contrast with what he has
just said to Mortimer, but which is not without its
effect.

The interview has the well-known result, and Leicester sees himself read through and through by Burleigh;
then, in order to crown his deeds, with nimble craft he
sacrifices Mortimer, the very man who wanted, magnani-
mously, to rescue him. He even sets the capstone upon
his treachery by insisting on the execution of the death-
penalty pronounced upon Mary. Here, however, his fate
overtakes him, announced by his adversary Burleigh's
words :

> "Since, then, his lordship shows such earnest zeal,
> Such loyalty, 'twere well were he appointed
> To see the execution of the sentence."

The nerves of the effeminate count were strong
enough to commit treachery, but they do not sustain
him in meeting its results. Mary, in saying to him—

> "You keep your word, my Lord of Leicester, for
> You promised me your arm to lead me forth
> From prison, and you lend it to me now"—

deservedly annihilates him. It is at this point that the
artist has caught him. The lord does, indeed, make an
effort to collect himself :

> "Wouldst thou not lose the guerdon of thy guilt
> Thou must uphold, complete it daringly.
> Pity be dumb, mine eyes be petrified;
> I'll see, I will be witness of her fall."

But the pangs of his conscience do not permit him to do so, and he falls in a swoon. It is his destiny that his repentance should have the same effect that his crime has ; after betraying. Mary by his double ~tongue, he betrays Elizabeth in his very remorse.

A peculiar .characteristic of all thoroughly base natures is, that, while regretting, indeed, all their evil deeds, they take all possible means to escape the results, instead of freely meeting the penalty of their own crimes ; and so Leicester ends in flight—true to his own character throughout the play—contemptible.

Mortimer

MORTIMER.

(*Mary Stuart.*)

WE have already repeatedly indicated, in our comments, that the characteristic which the German nation
especially values in Schiller, is his vigorous manfulness.
Nowhere is there to be detected in him a trace of that
singular mixture of cretinism and genius, not a trace
of that effeminateness which makes so many of our
artists of the second and third class appear like sick
oysters, whose artistic talent is their only pearl, and
whose weakly nature has contributed so much to the
popular belief that æsthetic endowment is, on the whole,
a kind of disease which necessarily makes its possessor
somewhat misshapen and unsound, or, at least, insipid.
In itself, however, the artistic faculty is nothing unnatural, nothing destructive of the harmonious wholeness
of a man, nothing that must weaken his energies ; on
the contrary, every great man has something of the
poet and the artist in himself, and perhaps they, most of
all, who, like generals and statesmen, are the farthest
removed from artist ranks.

The manly energy, the fresh spirit which have been exhibited in Mortimer, are the qualities which, in a measure, reconcile us to him, who has no other attributes calculated to awaken our interest, despite the seductive power of the language which the poet puts in his mouth, and which compels us all the more to express our views respecting his character as sharply as possible. Shorn of these advantages, almost every thing about him is ignoble. His characteristic quality is marked sensuality; not only his passion for Mary breathes the wildest ardor, but his going over to Catholicism is the result merely of the intoxication which the wonderful works of art, in Rome, have wrought upon his fanciful nature—Raphael's women, Palestrina's music, Michael Angelo's domes. He is, completely, a romanticist; it is not the germ of things that attracts him, it is the artistic form that infects him; so, directly after his religious conversion, he goes into merry society, passes from Romish ecclesiastical festivals to the "cheerful scenes of France," and ripens these for the cardinal, who—

"Showed me how the glimmering light of reason
Serves but to lead us to eternal error,
That what the heart is called on to believe
The eye must see."

But, if reason causes us thus to err, it is not clear why God has bestowed it; and it is no plume in the cap of Catholicism that it must surrender this faculty, however poetically the sacrifice may be presented to us.

Fanaticism and hypocrisy are twin-sisters, and so Mortimer makes, without delay, the acquaintance of the latter—unquestionably, the one most akin to the native reserve of an Englishman and his stubborn egotism. He learns the "difficult art of dissembling;" he does not even blush at confessing, before the whole court of England and his queen, that he has acted in a manner which, in common life, is called infamous; he even confesses that he has stolen into the confidence of the banished woman, and even made a pretence of surrendering his faith, in order to learn her purposes: "so far went my curiosity to serve thee" (Elizabeth)— a confession which, according to the opinions prevalent even then, would bring upon him the contempt of every man of honor. This he deserves, nevertheless, in spite of the want of truth in his confession, since it was entirely of a piece with all his conduct at the court of Elizabeth, and in relation to his own uncle. If this is reconcilable with honor, it is not clear where the bounds of the dishonorable begin.

Even Leicester, who, assuredly, was not a fool, deservedly says to him, in the scene in which the artist has portrayed him—

> "I see you, sir, exhibit at this court
> Two different aspects. One of them must be
> A borrowed one."

That his love to Mary, in like manner, has its source
. merely in sensuality, is everywhere shown us by the
poet, whether Mortimer tells her what impression her
picture made upon him, or confesses what impressions
she herself makes upon him :

> " Your prison's infamy !
> Hath it despoiled your beauty of its charms ?
> You are deprived of all that graces life,
> Yet round you life and light eternal beam."

Even to the last interview, where, with his immoderate
passion, he recalls to her her earlier amours, in order to
justify his claims to her favor, and demanding it, at last,
as the price of his service :

> " I will deliver you, and though it cost
> A thousand lives, I do it. But I swear,
> As God's in heaven, I will possess you too."

Elizabeth shows that she discerns his motives
with entire correctness, when she proposes to gain him
over by promising him her favor, repugnant as is this
touch of lechery in her ; and nothing justifies him in
saying—

> " Go, false, deceitful queen ! As thou deludest
> The world, e'en so I cozen thee. 'Tis right
> Thus to betray thee, 'tis a worthy deed ;
> Look I, then, like a murderer ? "—

and all the more, as directly afterward he shows that
she was not fair enough to recompense him for his
service ; whereas, without hesitation, he sacrifices every

thing that comes in his way for Mary; he is willing
even to murder his uncle, because—

> "*O'er her*, in rounds of endless glory, hover
> Spirits with grace and youth eternal blest,
> Celestial joy is throned upon her breast."

He has no superiority in morality, certainly, over
Leicester, he surpasses him merely in spirit and in
impudent daring ; and these qualities alone justify
Mortimer—at the time when Leicester asserts that an
effort to free Mary is not to be ventured upon—in
hurling at the latter this reproach :

> "Too hazardous for you who would possess her,
> But we, who only wish to rescue her,
> We are more bold."

This courageous spirit of youth reconciles us, in a
measure, to him, when he says—

> "A daring deed must one day end the matter,
> Why will you not with such a deed begin ?"—

or appeals to Mary :

> ' The coward loves his life. . . .
> Whoe'er would rescue you, and call you his,
> Must boldly dare affront e'en death itself."

It even glorifies his end, when, betrayed by Leicester,
he cries :

> "Infamous wretch ! But I deserve it all.
> Who told me, then, to trust this practised villain ? . . .
> Life is the faithless villain's only good."

24

We are never able wholly to withhold respect from him, who is ready to pledge even his life in behalf of his convictions, be they ever so false ; or actuated, as in Mortimer's case, by thoroughly egotistical motives.

BURLEIGH.

(*Mary Stuart.*)

IF a statesman is to be rightly judged, he must
not be viewed from the stand-point of private rights.
Above all things else, the time and the circumstances
amid which he lived must be made real. And so we
see Burleigh emerging amid the most envenomed civil
strifes, and, following him in his career, we see the
success which at last crowns his efforts, and those of
the queen, to give the realm a greatness hitherto
unknown, and to secure peace, in its outward relations,
at least; yet all his efforts are constantly imperilled by
the existence of a dangerous pretender to the crown.

If, in Schiller's tragedy, in the two queens, an exclusive predominance is given to the mere womanly
nature, the unatonable antagonism of two rivals, who
contend not only for a single throne, but no less for a
man loved by them both, we see in the lord treasurer
the cold representative of state-craft—the invincible
advocate of the Protestant party. The impression of
a certain measure of heartlessness in this one-sided

prominence, given to understanding and reason, is un-
avoidable, and Schiller has even intensified it by the
addition of legal subtlety : Burleigh hates, in Mary, the
Papist; in Leicester, the favorite of the queen. He is
completely indifferent in the choice of means, if he can
only attain his end—as much so as Mortimer on the
Catholic side. If, therefore, he appears to maintain,
strongly, the great principles of justice, which every
man may enjoy without distinction of person—

> " Where would be the state's
> Security, if the stern sword of justice .
> Could not as freely smite the guilty brow
> Of the imperial stranger as the beggar's ? "—

yet Mary justly describes him, as well as his method of
thinking, when she says to him, reproachfully, that, with
him, advantage weighs more than justice.

With cold blood he presses on as far as to the legal
murder of Mary; he would even be willing, in order to
be merely free of the disturber of the peace, to insti-
gate Paulet to become her assassin :

> " She scorns us, she defies us, will defy us,
> Even at the scaffold's foot. . . .
> The sword of justice which adorns the man
> Is hateful in a woman's hand. The world
> Will give no credit to a woman's justice,
> If woman be the victim. Vain that we,
> The judges, spoke what conscience dictated.
> She has the royal privilege of mercy,
> She must exert it. 'Twere not to be borne,

Should she let justice take its full career;
Therefore, should she yet live? Oh, no,
She must not live, it must not be; 'tis this,
Even this, my friend, that so disturbs the queen.
. . . .
Well might it be avoided, thinks the queen,
If she had only more attentive servants.
. . . .
Who, when a poisonous adder is delivered
Into their hands, would keep the treacherous charge,
As if it were a sacred, precious jewel?"

There is something that reminds us of the old Cato's
" Ceterum censeo," when we see the fixed, resolute man
continually coming back, with fearful steadfastness of purpose, to his demand for the death of the Scottish queen—

" They demand
The Stuart's head. If to thy people thou
Wouldst now secure the precious boon of freedom,
And the fair light of truth so dearly won,
Then she must die. If we are not to live
In endless terror for thy precious life,
The enemy must fall. . . .
No peace can be with her and with her house.
Thou must resolve to strike or suffer;
Her life is death to thee—her death thy life"—

when he seeks to put out of the way every thing which
could hinder the attainment of this goal, and, among
others, the interview of Elizabeth and Mary—

"For her, the base encourager of murder,
Her who hath thirsted for our sovereign's blood,
The privilege to see the royal presence
Is forfeited. . . .

> She is condemned to death, her head is laid
> Beneath the axe, and it would ill become
> The queen to see a death-devoted head.
> The sentence cannot have its execution
> If the queen's majesty approaches her,
> For pardon still attends the royal presence "—

and when, at last, after the unhappy result of the interview, and the attempt upon the queen's life, he believes the opportunity come to carry the sentence into execution, he hastens, with the utmost speed, to take advantage of Elizabeth's passionate excitement. Burleigh's decided character shows itself most in the scenes with the French ambassador, and with Leicester, whose artifices he quickly sees through, overwhelming him with cutting scorn; and, with cool villany, compelling him to be the very man appointed to lead Mary to her execution:

> "This same Mortimer
> Died most conveniently for you, my lord.
> .   .   .   .
> Since, then, his lordship shows such earnest zeal—
> Such loyalty, 'twere well were he appointed
> To see the execution of the sentence."

The vast superiority of the statesman's reasoning is shown in marked contrast with that of other men around him, who are impelled by their private passions merely, in the scene where Elizabeth hesitates to sign the death-warrant. From the moment when he says to her—

> "Obey thy people's voice, it is the voice of God "—

and sets aside Shrewsbury's objection that the queen,
in her present humor, was not master of her own
judgment—

"Judgment has long been passed, it is not now"—

down to the time when, with a frankness and a
vehemence which only the consciousness of being the
representative of a great principle can give, he holds up
her duties to the queen—

"Wait for it, pause, delay, till flames of fire
Consume the realm, until the fifth attempt
Of murder be successful! God, indeed,
Hath thrice delivered thee. Thy late escape
Was marvellous, and to expect again
A miracle would be to tempt thy God. . . .
You say you love your people 'bove yourself—
Now prove it. Choose not peace for your own heart,
And leave your kingdom to the storms of discord.
Think on the Church. Shall, with this Papist queen,
The ancient superstition be renewed?
The monk resume his sway, the Roman legate
In pomp march hither, lock our churches up,
Dethrone our monarchs? I demand of you
The souls of all your subjects; as you now
Shall act, they all are saved or all are lost.
Here is no time for mercy; to promote
Your people's welfare is your highest duty.
If Shrewsbury has saved your life, then I
Will save both you and England, that is more"—

and, with these words, regains the esteem which his
apparent heartlessness withdrew from him, since we see

that personal motives do not actuate him, but that the
welfare of his country is the highest spur to all his
actions. This nobler, grander sense of obligation does
not take away from him the stiff, unbending air with
which he brings the death-sentence to Mary, and receives
her last wishes—the moment in which the artist has
represented him.

Ph. D. Sr. del.   R. Goldberg sculp.

Joan.

JOAN.

(*The Maid of Orleans.*)

So unrivalled is the place that this enthusiastic girl occupies in history, that, on that very account, she is even at this present time an object of contemplation and of wonder for the statesman and politician, as well as of the devotion and the completely justified reverence of every sensitive heart. All the explanations which have been made of this remarkable episode in French history have served, not only to increase the impression of astonishment, but also to perfectly justify Schiller's conception of Joan, and have been steadfastly opposed to the really obnoxious manner in which a few of her own countrymen have made her a subject of the most frivolous wit and the most common ribaldry. Voltaire, in especial, has exhibited a conspicuous instance of his low tone of thought in his notorious " Pucelle."

Recent historical investigations confirm, as before remarked, Schiller's representation of the youth and the probable solitary training of the maid. We meet her in the seclusion of shepherd-life; whose isolation

25

so strongly tempts the spirit to contemplation, to deep introversion, to fanaticism; and, in this retired life, she has become capable of that lofty enthusiasm and that glow of ecstasy which she exhibits; she has, moreover, been driven to the necessity of cultivating the utmost courage of spirit, in consequence of her defencelessness in the wild haunts which she frequented. She delights in her youthful years, and in her blossoming beauty; she has just entered the age which is decisive with her destiny as a maid—the age when that impulse awakens, which either finds its fulfilment in love, as is the case with most women, or, as sometimes occurs, which prompts one to follow some ideal interest, ordinarily that of religion. With Joan's lofty spirit, the choice must be the latter; an inclination to undertake a mission, and even the appearing of visions, were what would be expected in such a soul; and, unquestionably, a person in her condition would necessarily take hold of that which most moved her being. That, at her time, the dull roar of the tempests, that were raging through her native land, at length penetrated her ear too, and filled her heart with fierce hatred against the cruel oppressors, is perfectly comprehensible; and no less so is the immense effect which it could awaken in this spirit, which was only seeking an occasion to call out its latent enthusiasm.

Upon this simple and colossal nature the thought of her country's need fell like a spark, that set her whole soul on fire. A worthy goal had only been wanted to raise her soul to the greatest ecstasy, in which she must seem like a riddle to her relatives, whose souls were not capable of a like impulse. To a spirit highly stimulated, and naturally heroic, the wish to attempt the delivery of her country was not so far removed, but that dreams and visions in the night should seem to make the deliverance of the nation a call of duty.

That the sudden appearance of the enthusiastic maid amid a people which, at every time, is capable of passing from extreme depression to the greatest enthusiasm, and the reverse, must have kindled the popular zeal all the more, if she emerged into public view at the time when the national hopelessness, begotten by the indecisive bearing of the king, had reached the highest point; and when the nation, discouraged by long misfortune, exasperated to the utmost by oppression, could say to itself—

> "Worthless is the nation that stakes not
> Its all with cheerfulness upon its honor"—

that her appearance should effect all this, although remarkable and interesting in the highest degree, is by no means explicable.

On the contrary, that, at the first surprise of the nation, she could effect that transformation into an enthusiasm which overcame every thing in its way, is all the more clear, from the fact that numerous prophecies had prepared the minds, not only of the masses, but also of scholars, to expect such a wonderful phenomenon as her appearance. But, in Joan's feeling at the same time that, by this warlike mission, she was stepping out of the circle imposed upon her by virtue of her sex, the thought suggests itself at once to her, in full accordance with the spirit of her age, that this step is only to be atoned by renouncing earthly love, as one consecrated to God. Moreover, it is a confident belief in her mission which is displayed, when she feels herself pledged to spare no enemy, and strikes down young Montgomery without any compunctions of conscience; and so, too, when, confronting him, she utters her belief in her obligation to show no mercy—

> "I'm born a shepherd-maid.
> This hand, accustomed to the peaceful crook,
> Is all unused to wield the sword of death.
> Yet, snatched away from childhood's peaceful haunts,
> From the fond love of father and of sisters,
> Urged by no idle dream of earthly glory,
> But Heaven-appointed to achieve your ruin,
> Like a destroying angel I must roam,
> Spreading dire havoc round me, and, at length,
> Myself must fall a sacrifice to death.
> Never again shall I behold my home:"—

and so she feels, too, after passing so completely and irrevocably from the wonted place of woman, that she cannot return thither, that she must not only sacrifice victims, but be one herself. But when this self-denying, womanly heart asserts its rights, when, at Lionel's glance, love approaches her, this feeling confuses her, and appears to her a crime :

> " What ! I permit a human form
>   To haunt my bosom's sacred cell,
>   And there, where heavenly radiance shone,
>   Doth earthly love presume to dwell ?
>   The savior of my country, I,
>   The warrior of God most high,
>   Burn for my country's foeman ? "

All intense excitement, like that which carried Joan away, and the people with her, gives place to a sense of satiety and exhaustion when its goal is reached, and, as a result of this necessary reaction, we have to view what occurred after the entry into Rheims—the accusation of her own father, and the ingratitude of the court. Meantime, Joan's own consciousness of guilt prevents her quickly replying to the accusations urged, and permits her to doubt as to the validity of her own mission, and at the very instant when the result of her heroism was most triumphantly displayed. The reason was, that after having once renounced nature, she felt that the return to it would be a contradiction—a want of loyalty. Perceiving this satiety and exhaustion around her, she doubts still more about herself; what had just appeared to her as a calling from God, seems to her now, if not a delusion of the devil, yet, at least, a trial which she must bear as a penance.

Like the whole nation, she, too, finds her faith in

her high mission return to her, in its full strength, when pressing need approaches anew ; her old enthusiasm overcomes her afresh, leading her to victory and to death, and causing her to utter once more the feeling of regained harmony with herself :

> " No, I am not a sorceress ! Indeed
> I am not one. . . .
> Yes, all around me now seems clear again :
> That is my king ; these banners, here, of France ;
> My banner I behold not. Where is it ?
> Without my banner I dare not appear ;
> To me it was confided by my Lord,
> And I before His throne must lay it down.
> I there may show it, for I bore it truly."

Fr. Pecht del.   L. Sichling sculp.

...in ever being conquered, but is in full
danger when a king takes it to the
...in peaceful times, but amid wild, warlike
...demand a whole man, and find nothing
but being weakling.

VII. as Schiller, closely following history,
such a dilettante king very "respect

CHARLES VII.

DILETTANTEISM is everywhere repugnant, but it is full of profoundest danger when a king takes it to the throne, not in peaceful times, but amid wild, warlike times, which demand a whole man, and find nothing but an art-loving weakling.

Charles VIL, as Schiller, closely following history, pictures him, is such a dilettante king; very "respectable" and well brought up, he never does any thing ungracefully; having a fine gift of language, he always makes beautiful speeches, full of delicate fancy, when actions are wanted; he wishes well to every thing, but has power for nothing. Take hold of him firmly, and he shrinks back. He is like snow, that never holds an impression, and melts in your hands when you think you have secured it. For all his gentle, good wishes, of which he is full; for all his sighs and moans over the misery of his country, he is still able to keep himself in the best possible condition—he makes verses, he has them sung before him; he loves artists and hates soldiers,

Were he deprived of his artist friends, he would certainly love soldiers, for, at bottom, it is a sense of duty
which is hateful to him; he wants mere pleasures; he
would like to make his people happy, yet without any
effort of his own. Like all weak natures, he lays great
stress on external appearances; a prescribed form must
make up for hollowness within; nothing is so repugnant
to him as Dunois's rough modes of speech; had court
etiquette not been invented long ago, he would certainly
have brought it into vogue, in order to keep himself free
from every thing that might disturb his sentimental and
romantic inclinations. So, when he first comes before
us, he is glad to be free of the Connétable; his joy at
this far surpasses the humiliation and the pain of surrendering all his territory as far as to the Loire. On
this account, too, is love so important to him, and Agnes
so dear; she supports him without knowing it, and he
finds it charming that she offers every thing to him,
even her honor, and will receive nothing from him but
his love.

It is perfectly comprehensible how such a character,
at the head of a nation, can completely demoralize it,
since it cannot drop him with all the good-nature that
he seems to have; and yet, while despairing about its
head, it at last loses confidence in the power of the
limbs, and so falls into that discouraged and pitiable
condition in which we find it at the commencement of
the play, and out of which the spectacle of Joan's brave

spirit quickly plucks it. Even Charles has occasional traces of a knightly temper—where they are not especially becoming; in one of these he calls out the Duke of Burgundy, in the assured conviction that the challenge will not be accepted. It was only a romantic flight of his; for, directly after, when the national danger was at the highest, he shows himself completely destitute of resources, breaks down utterly, and tries to comfort himself for his want of spirit with the words:

> "A dark and ominous doom
> Impendeth o'er the Heaven-abandoned house
> Of Valois. There preside the avenging powers,
> To whom a mother's crimes unbarred the way."

After the manner of such natures, he quickly and with skilful instinct transfers his own faults to the shoulders of others.

Can we find reason to wonder that the forceful queen Isabeau — that proud, manlike woman — despises this "respectable," art-loving son? She has too well experienced the perfidy which is the constant companion of such weak natures as are never able to hold firmly to any thing. How little Charles understands this, we see in the readiness with which he will surrender Orleans; and when Dunois represents to him that they are all ready to espouse his cause, for—

> "It is the law of destiny that nations
> Should, for their monarchs, immolate themselves.

26

> We Frenchmen recognize this sacred law,
> Nor would annul it"—

he yet gives all up; and answers—

> "I can do no more"—

and comforts himself like the dilettante he is, who
always leaves in the lurch the call of duty when
difficulties come :

> "Is, then, the sceptre such a peerless treasure?
> Is it so hard to loose it from our grasp?"

If, as a king, he always falls short, it cannot be
denied that he possesses many of the virtues of a private
man ; he is good-humored, free-handed, full of fine
fantasies; without being brilliant or deep, he has much
tender feeling, as exhibited in the difficult scene of the
Duke of Burgundy, and in the gentleness that would
remove every thing that might wound the newly-won
friend.   Everywhere he shows himself easily propitiated ;
he does not hold firmly to any thoughts of vengeance—
for the reason, perhaps, that he does not hold firmly
to any thing.   All that remains constant to him, in
all circumstances, is his glibness of speech.   Crowned
romanticists always know how to make very fine and
intellectual observations, particularly about things that
are past and gone.   They are the true funeral preachers ;
and King Charles shows himself a master of this craft,
when he says of the dead Talbot:

"Well, peace be with his ashes. Bear him hence.
 Here, in the heart of France, where his career
 Of conquest ended, let his relics lie.
 So far no hostile sword attained before.
 A fitting tomb shall memorize his name,
 His epitaph the spot whereon he fell."

Nothing better, surely, could be said regarding the hero, after he had been so badly fought with! ·

But, if he knows how to do justice to the dead, his want of ability to do so with the living becomes the more conspicuous. We have an instance of this in the coronation scene, where he proposes to raise an altar to the maiden who has won for him his crown and realm, and put her by the side of St. Denis, and then, ten minutes later, at the accusation of a bigoted peasant, he lets her stand helpless, and even carries his favor so far that he, who owes her every thing, says through the lips of Du Chatel:

"Joanna d'Arc, uninjured from the town
 The king permits you to depart. The gates
 Stand open to you; fear no injury,
 You are protected by the royal word."

Of course, our artistic king does not let the opportunity slip of pronouncing a funeral discourse upon her, after she had died for him:

"She's gone, she never will awaken more;
 Her eye will gaze no more on earthly things.
 She soars on high, a spirit glorified;
 She seeth not our grief—our penitence."

This completes the picture of his weakness. His feeble nature cannot fail to be discerned in our drawing, based, as it is, upon existing portraits; in the narrow face, the great, dreamy eyes, the long, thin nose, the sharp lips, and the little, thin hand, as well as in the slender, effeminate figure, it is only too plainly expressed. Seizing Charles's character, where most clearly developed in the play, the artist has represented him in the scene where, just before the appearance of the maid, he gives up his cause in despair, and sighs—

"Blood hath been poured forth freely, and in vain.
The hand of Heaven is visibly against me."

Fr Pecht del.   A. Schultheiss sculp.

AGNES SOREL.

(*The Maid of Orleans.*)

THE genius of woman lies in her heart, and when the demands of the heart are completely satisfied, we must study woman's affectional nature only in its own appropriate realm, and find some new surprise in its inexhaustible supply of features which move and touch us.

Such a character — which has enjoyed the good fortune of remaining in perfect harmony with itself, notwithstanding that it has been adorned, not only with all personal charms, but also with those of uncommon intellectual power, as well as of superior education—we see in the renowned woman, whose pure and exalted love, for ages beautified with all the charm of romance, has assumed a worthy place in all souls capable of feeling, and to whom our Schiller also has erected a fair memorial in his work, investing that tenderness of hers, which has become proverbial, with all the magical charms of his poesy. In his production, we become acquainted with her as one of the most conspicuous priestesses of love, as that one of all his heroines who has lived most exclusively to love alone.

The laws of the realm making it difficult for the king to give a priestly consecration to the alliance which his heart had formed with her, and compelling him, would he do this, to descend from his royal position, and deny legitimacy to his heirs, she is unwilling to accept this sacrifice, although it is offered to her, and although her illicit relation to him brings a blemish upon·her, of which she shows herself to be perfectly conscious, when she says to him :

> "How! Have I freely sacrificed to thee
> What is esteemed far more than gold or pearls,
> And shall I now hold back the gifts of fortune?"

She knows that she can only make the want of position good by unbounded fidelity and devotion, and therefore she makes the further sacrifice of her wealth, not only without hesitation, but she even refuses to appropriate every temporary advantage which she might draw from the king's passion for her. Yet he himself says of her :

> "She's nobly born as I—
> The royal blood of Valois not more pure ;
> The most exalted throne she would adorn,
> Yet she rejects it with disdain, and claims
> No other title than to be my love.
> No gift more costly will she e'er receive ·
> Than early flower in winter or rare fruit,
> No sacrifice on my part she permits,

Yet sacrificeth all she hath to me.
With generous spirit she doth venture all—
Her wealth and fortune—in my sinking bark."

While she claims nothing for herself but the right to sacrifice every thing for him—that fairest and most charming right of all tender, womanly hearts—she yet neglects no means to call back to the weak man's remembrance his duty as king; she spares no pains in keeping him secure in his exalted place. She appeals to him—

"Thy courtiers metamorphose into soldiers,
Thy gold transmute to iron. All thou hast,
With resolute daring, venture for thy crown"—

and still displays the noblest spirit when misfortune has mounted to the highest point, and when he, in his pusillanimity, is ready to renounce all; she buoys him up, with a hero's spirit, when he gives way:

"God forbid
That we, in weak despair, should quit this realm!
This utterance came not from thy heart, my king—
Thy noble heart, which hath been sorely riven
By the fell deed of thy unnatural mother.
Thou'lt be thyself again. Right valiantly
Thou'lt battle with thine adverse destiny,
Which doth oppose thee with relentless ire."

She reveals to us a great, noble soul, which only her own wealth of love deceives respecting. the weakness of her lover, to whom her fancy lends all the advantages, the want of which makes him play so sorry a part. She

feels rightly, as only love can feel, that if a miracle alone
can carry him through the tempest of fierce battle, he
has such a good-will to his people, and such a noble disposition, that he will be able to bless his land when once
it is in peace:

> " Heaven, in thy gentle spirit, hath prepared
> The leech to remedy the thousand ills
> By party rage inflicted on the land.
> The flames of civil discord thou wilt quench,
> And my heart tells me thou'lt establish peace,
> And found anew the monarchy of France."

The humbleness and modesty which the fair lady
shows on every occasion, the bashful manner with
which she offers her jewels—in which act the artist
represents her to us—as well as the veneration with
which she throws herself in the dust before Joan—
in all these she appears as the gentle, affectionate, devoted creature to whom love is all.   On this account,
too, she cannot comprehend the Maid of Orleans ; she
cannot understand a mission which shall, after the goal
of battle is reached, close the heart to those gentle
emotions which she experiences, and therefore says
to her—

> " Oh ! couldst thou own a woman's feeling heart !
> Put off this armor, war is over now ;
> Confess thy union with the softer sex.
> My loving heart shrinks timidly from thee,
> While thus thou wearest Pallas' brow severe "—

where she would gladly see Joan share the rapture

which she feels, and which she expresses so naive and humanly :

> " For—all my weakness shall I own to thee ?
> Not the renown of France, my fatherland,
> Not the new splendor of the monarch's crown,
> Not the triumphant gladness of the crowds,
> Engage this woman's heart. One only form
> Is in its depths enshrined. It hath not room
> For any feeling save for one alone.
> He is the idol—him the people bless,
> Him they extol, for him they strew these flowers ;
> And he is mine—he is my own true love."

The fate of the historical Sorel was what would be expected from linking her destiny to a character so weak as Charles : weary of the court, or herself grown superfluous there, she withdrew to her palace Beauté, from which she received the name " Dame de Beauté." At the repeated invitation of the king and queen, however, she visited the palace once more, where, in 1450, she suddenly died, as was suspected, from poison.

The picture which we give of her is based upon an authentic portrait coming down from her time, which suffers us to suspect the gentle and devoted character of the fair lady, to whose soft heart love could lend every thing, and which it was even able to steel with courage and decision.

27

TALBOT.

(*The Maid of Orleans.*)

If in the Maid we have the power of faith personified, and see it victorious over every thing — all material forces, all the appliances of the understanding, the art of war as well as state-craft, if these all are able to effect nothing when brought into collision with faith's immeasurable power, we need, as a representative of these resistant forces, one who shall bring out their entire possibility into the clearest light, and make their triumph all the more brilliant.

This contrast to the Maid is presented in Talbot, who possesses every thing in profusion which is lacking to the inexperienced Joan: the richest experience, the confident self-consciousness of a victorious general, a truly colossal mind, an invincible, all-defying courage, unfailing presence of mind, and all these qualities interpenetrated by the keenest understanding, in which he stands far before all the other characters of the great scene. But this very pitiless logic of thought, in the unbending hero-nature that is so imposing, is powerless

against the enthusiasm of faith; for, while this binds
together what is most widely sundered, and melts, with
its glow, the stiff ice-covering of brittle natures, that
cutting sharpness often separates and isolates, instead
of binding together.

This portentous working of his spirit we learn at
the very first appearance of the general. With entire
correctness he declares the panic of the soldiers to be
folly; but he pains the allies at the same time, by
giving prominence to his most marked characteristics
—his genuine English pride, hardness, and relentlessness.
In reading the contest-scene with the Duke of Burgundy,
our thoughts are transferred, involuntarily, to much later
times. Controlled, as he was, by understanding alone,
Talbot must always give weight to those reasons and
convictions which, with the mass of men, have so little
weight; and, therefore, repugnant as Queen Isabeau
is to his nature, he yet bows before her mind, and
gives her, despite his pride, the hand of reconciliation.
Notwithstanding, while he yields to her reasoning, he
cannot deny himself the satisfaction of repaying this
humiliation by giving Queen Isabeau a few malicious
side-thrusts :

> "Go, in God's name! When you have left the camp,
> No devil will again appall our troops."

How the sword-like sharpness of his nature appears in
every word!

There follow the two battles, whose description is

among the finest which Schiller's muse has given to us, and in which we see the hero submit to the most searching trial. It is a perfectly correct touch, that he alone remains unconfused in the universal panic, yet his nature being, as it is, simply under the control of understanding, does not enable him to comprehend the tumultuous fear that prevails; he does not understand the wondrous power that confronts him; to him the Maid is merely—

> " The juggling minx who plays the well-learned part
> Of heroine."

We pardon him for this one-sidedness merely out of regard to the heroic defiance with which, amid the universal panic, he swears:

> " This sword shall pierce
> Who talks to me of fear or coward flight ! "

This interest in the proud hero is yet heightened when we fall in with him the third time; conquered and mortally wounded, we hear him, in his pain and despair, curse, like the bound Prometheus, that fate which he regards as unjust; and, with dreadful energy, he breaks out into the celebrated words:

> " Folly, thou conquerest, and I must yield.
> Against stupidity the very gods
> Themselves contend in vain. Exalted Reason,
> Resplendent daughter of the Head divine,
> Wise foundress of the system of the world,

> Guide of the stars, who art thou then, if thou,
> Bound to the tail of Folly's uncurbed steed,
> Must, vainly shrieking, with the drunken crowd,
> Eyes open, plunge down headlong in the abyss?"

This blasphemy works all the more powerfully and fearfully upon us, since the nature of the man, who gives vent to it, has become so clear, that we see that this feeling has sprung necessarily out of his very soul.

The whole lofty, proud grief of this vanquished spirit lies in his wrath as he continues :

> " Accursed who striveth after noble ends,
> And with deliberate wisdom forms his plans !
> To the fool-king belongs the world."

Nor can we refuse to justify his point of view when he says :

> " But to be baffled by such juggling arts !
> Deserved our earnest and laborious life
> Not a more earnest issue ? "—

on the contrary, we admire the genuineness, heroism, brevity, and nervousness of this dying speech, that grand contempt of all pathos, that proud modesty with which he calls his fame - crowned life merely " earnest and laborious." It is, therefore, a really tragic event that the limitations of his nature and his want of fantasy allow him no bridge to the world beyond — a world which not the intellect grasps, but the soul perceives; so that he, who fills the world with his warlike name, carries from the strife of life no other booty than—

"an insight into nothingness,
And utter scorn of all which once appeared
To us exalted and desirable."

In this cold view something colossal appears to us to exist. Notwithstanding that we are convinced of his grievous error, and see perfectly clearly that he must rightly succumb, because, in the pride of his own power, he despises the heart of man—the inexhaustible source of feeling; and, in his blindness, does not perceive that that which he has lightly undertaken is an attack upon the existence of a noble race, before whose wounded pride all individual superiority must succumb—despite all this, we admire the hero still.

There is something Napoleonic in this nature, in this energetic realism which fails to recognize ideal forces, even then, when, vanquished by them, he is cast down to the earth.

Fr Pecht del.   IL. Merz s

QUEEN ISABEAU.

(The Maid of Orleans.)

THERE is no figure in the drama so well adapted to bring home to us the disturbed condition of affairs in all France at that time, to show us how completely all natural bonds were severed during the civil war, as that of the queen, who goes so far beyond the limits prescribed by her sex, and who forms in her whole aspect so fearful a contrast to the Maid. She is thoroughly adapted to prepare us for the extraordinary apparition which we are subsequently to encounter in Joan. If the latter renounces her womanly nature out of devotion to a loftier idea, Isabeau, impelled by a wild passion, acts in equal disregard and defiance of her position as wife and mother.

To account for a psychological process so abnormal, needs little more than to cite the points in her character, given slightly and sketchily in the play, yet with masterly correctness. At the outset we see nothing but the fear and dismay which this woman's unnatural warfare with her own son excites in the mass of men; and with these

28

we discern the opposition which is encountered even
from the more highly-trained generals, who frankly say :

> " Go ! go ! The thought of combatting for you
> Unnerves the courage of the bravest men."

Yet even they yield to the force of the reasons which
this clever woman urges, and unite, after a most bitter
feud had parted them ! In the brief, masterly scene,
which is allowed her for her justification, she quickly
displays all the qualities which the artist needs to use in
drawing her portrait ; and it is here, therefore, that she
is represented. She shows us there the richly-endowed,
proud, mighty nature, with its penetrating understanding,
and strong, eager sensuousness ; with her, feeling has but
a subordinate part to play. Had this spirited, heroic,
commanding princess had a husband who was her equal,
sound in mind and in body—in one word, a true man—
she would assuredly never have gone beyond the circle
which her sex and the habits of her age prescribed.
But, in her very youth, she is compelled to enter into
the most unnatural relations—thrust into a foreign land,
compelled to marry a man at whose side she experiences,
not rapture, but compassion or fear. And now the fierce,
uncontrolled elements in her character break forth ; she
herself says :

> " I've passions and warm blood, and, as a queen,
> Come to this realm to live, and not to seem.
> Should I have lingered out a joyless life
> Because the curse of adverse destiny

> To a mad consort joined my blooming youth?
> More than my life I prize my liberty;
> And who assails me here "—

Her inborn trustfulness—

> "Hypocrisy I scorn. Such as I am,
> So let the world behold me "—

now becomes arrogance, just as the nature of woman, inclined as it is to follow, to cling, to obey, is brought to do the very reverse, when deprived of the conditions necessary to its free development. It is so here, where a young, fair, richly-gifted princess is deprived of one who ought to be her lord, and sees herself surrounded only by subjects and flatterers. If this necessary environment of princes fills her fiery, penetrating spirit with depreciation of other men, the character of her own son must do so still more. At the outset she despises in him the weakling, the characterless, fluctuating mind, which can hold firmly to nothing, which can neither love nor hate heartily, and which is therefore always untrue. This feeling we gather from her expressions when she takes the Maid captive, and learns of her that she has been banished by the dauphin:

> "Banished—because you save him from the abyss;
> Banished! therein I recognize my son!"

This well-deserved contempt is gradually transformed into intense hate, when this weakling, who is so infinitely surpassed by his mother in understanding, courage, and

vigor, undertakes to be her lord and master—to judge
her morals, and to banish her. Then, for the first time,
wounded in her inmost soul, with her passionate, choleric
temperament, shrinking back from nothing, she curses
him :

> "Your feeble nature cannot comprehend
> The vengeance of an outraged mother's heart.
> Who pleases me, I love ; who wrongs, I hate.
> If he who wrongs me chance to be my son,
> All the more worthy is he of my hate.
> The life I gave, I will again take back
> From him who doth, with ruthless violence,
> The bosom rend which bore and nourished him.
> Ye who do thus make war upon the dauphin,
> What rightful cause have ye to plunder him ?
> What crime hath he committed against you ?
> What insult are you called on to avenge ?
> Ambition, paltry envy, goad you on ;
> I have a right to hate him—he's my son."

After preserving her courage to the latest moment,
not giving up, even when all around her have fled,
steadfast in her hate, as, under other circumstances, she
would have been in her love, she has nothing more to
hope for than not to meet, when vanquished, the object
of her aversion—

> "Every place
> The same where I encounter not the dauphin"—

and passes from view, filling us, if not with respect, at
least with a timid awe of her greatness, and the Titanic
wildness and vigor of her nature, and mingling these
with amazement and admiration.

There are several portraits of this notable woman in existence, one of which, to be seen in the gallery of Versailles, has been used by the artist as the foundation of his drawing. Although it represents her soon after her marriage, it yet enables us to detect the energy and strong sensuousness which were so marked elements in her character.

A v. Ramberg del.   Ad. Neumann sculp.

Donna Isabella

DONNA ISABELLA.

(*The Bride of Messina.*)

ALL art must bear a national stamp; its works must correspond to the habits, manners, and character of the people from which they spring—must reflect it in its individuality, although ennobled in form and substance, if its full effect is to be attained, and the public welfare be benefited. Beginning with this principle, we may easily understand why "The Bride of Messina," in spite of the wondrous fineness of its diction, and the extreme dignity and loftiness of its thought, is the one of all Schiller's pieces which has had the least influence, and least completely domesticated itself in Germany. It is the foreign aspect of the form as well as of the ideas which causes this play to appear as a more or less exotic plant. If, at this time, we wonder at the path which Schiller struck out in "The Bride of Messina," we ought not to forget that he and Goethe, at their appearance, found in their nation no high culture, no firmly-settled taste, and no répertoire worth the name, if we except a

few pieces of Lessing. They were, consequently, given
to experiments, and, as is well known, gradually passed
from the imitation of Shakespeare to the Greek tragedy
—a course which> every scholar takes once, and then
returns to the modern form.

The greatest and the most venturesome of the novel-
ties which Schiller attempts, in " The Bride of Messina,"
is the introduction of the moralizing chorus, as a kind
of personified public opinion. Still it is not perfectly
intelligible to us, although Schiller, by dividing it into
two parts, and giving several leaders to them, makes
important concessions to modern taste. Schiller, according to his own confession, wanted to transfer the plot of
his piece to an ideal time, and give it the simplest form
of life, in order that it should be purely human ; in·this
way he believed that he should lift tragedy into a higher
sphere, giving it that Greek form which appeared to
him the purest and most ideal. But Greek art is. the
most national of all, and its forms are therefore never
perfectly intelligible in a time so different and in a
world so different as our own. He was compelled,
at the .outset, to make concessions to modern feeling,
as already ·said, with· respect · to the choir, and also
to give· his characters certain special features which
do not belong to all time, but to a certain definite
period.

The poet had, unquestionably, in mind the Norman
conquerors of Sicily, when he painted the royal family,

whose turbulent passions bring them to so tragic an end.
The finger-marks of this are so abundant in the play,
that there can be scarcely a doubt of it. Isabella, for
example, says to her sons, directly after the first meeting
of their retinues :

> "What could have been their real interest with you—
> The foreigners, the race that violently claims the soil,
> Driving the ancient lords from their own heritage,
> And claiming precedence before them?"

The artist has, accordingly, adopted the costume of
the eleventh century — the flourishing epoch of that
Roman-Byzantine style, which, in Sicily, assumed so
peculiar a form by the intermingling of marked Sara-
cenic elements, left behind them by the former lords of
the land. Schiller, everywhere, lays special emphasis
upon these Moorish constituents of Messina, and still
more the remains of old heathen ideas; we hear of
the gods as much as we do of the Church, and
the Mohammedan belief in destiny as well as the Pagan
trust in oracles are intermingled with Christian tradi-
tions.

Upon this background now appears the imposing
figure of Donna Isabella, consecrating her deep grief
over her departed, heroic husband. The dark veil of
a heavy sorrow only makes more conspicuous in her
noble figure the loftiness of soul which she everywhere
displays, that grandeur and acuteness of spirit which the
chorus paints with the words:

29

> "Yes, there is something great, I must respect it,
> In a potentate's princely thought,
> And upon human action and dealings
> Looks she with peaceful calmness down."

This nobleness is the first thing that strikes us, but not less clearly is the instinct for rule displayed ; the preservation of her realm for her race she never loses from sight a moment.   Schiller is our only poet who everywhere impresses upon his characters greatness and dignity, and the seal of power.   This most difficult of all art-problems he has the skill to solve everywhere, and, in Donna Isabella, we find a recurrence of those qualities which win our astonishment in Wallenstein, Elizabeth of England, Mary Stuart, Philip II., and others.   The manner in which the pain-stricken mother makes her sons conscious of their equal deserts, the manner with which she portrays to them the dreadful picture of the necessary results of their feud, shows us not only her greatness, but also that tremendous passionateness to which, one after another, all the members of her house fall as victims.   She has her share in misfortune, as that excess of pride teaches us she must have, where, informed about her sons' love, she cries :

> "Oh, happiest mother! Chief of women!
> In bliss supreme! can aught of earthly joy
> O'erbalance thine?"

With wonderful poetic power and sustained strength

the chorus warns against such exaggerated feeling by
the uncovered corpse of Don Manuel:

> " When clouds athwart the lowering sky
> Are driven—when bursts of hollow moan
> The thunder's peal—our trembling bosoms own
> The might of awful Destiny!
> Yet oft the lightning's glare
> Darts sudden through the cloudless air;—
> Then in thy short, delusive day
> Of bliss, oh! dread the treacherous snare;
> Nor prize the fleeting goods and vain,
> The flowers that bloom but to decay!
> Nor wealth, nor joy, nor aught but pain,
> Was e'er to mortal's lot secure;
> Our first, best lesson—to endure!"

In vain! for by this corpse she at once, in the outbreak
of her boundless passion, curses his murderer's whole
race, and even turns her angry cries against Heaven—

> "And is it thus
> Ye keep your word, ye gods? Is this your truth?
> Alas! for him that trusts with honest heart
> Your soothing wiles. . . .
> Why do we lift
> Our suppliant hands, and at the sacred shrines
> Kneel to adore? Good, easy dupes, what win we
> From faith and pious awe? . . .
> The book of Nature is a maze, a dream
> The sage's art, and every sign a falsehood!"—

and, at the very height of her despair, she still
gives utterance to the proud, unbending spirit—the

fundamental cause of the overthrow of the whole
royal house:

> "The gods have done their worst. If they be true
> Or false, 'tis one, for nothing they can add
> To this; the measure of their rage is full.
> Why should I tremble, that have naught to fear?"

DON MANUEL.

(*The Bride of Messina.*)

By quoting a few sentences from Schiller's remarkable introduction to "The Bride of Messina," we shall give the reader the best view of the poet's conception of what is the true foundation of all works of art:

"Art has for its object not merely a transient pleasure to excite to a momentary dream of liberty. Its aim is to make us absolutely free; and this it accomplishes by awakening, exercising, and perfecting in us a power to remove to an objective distance the sensible world, to transform it into the free working of our spirit, and thus acquire a dominion over the material by means of ideas. For the very reason, also, that true art requires something of the objective and real, it is not satisfied with the show of truth. It rears its ideal edifice on truth itself—on the solid and deep foundations of nature."

While the poet makes this demand—that the artist thoroughly idealize nature, "transform it into the free working of his spirit"—in other words, omit all that does not belong to the idea of his work, but supply all that is wanting to make it complete—it is presupposed that, as in the whole, so in each particular character, he begins with a certain definite conception of nature, and merely beautifies. and ennobles it through the medium of a poetic spirit.   In " The Bride of Messina," however, he takes a -long step beyond this theory, as well as beyond his wont in other plays.   This he indicates in the next sentence :

"But how art can be at once altogether ideal, yet, in the strictest sense, real; how it can entirely leave the actual, and yet harmonize with nature, is a problem to the multitude."

In order to solve this problem, he substitutes here for that view of nature—which is exalted into .an ideal.—an ideal to which merely the forms and the organisms of nature are lent—that is to say, he strikes out an entirely new and untried path ; for all his other figures, from Fiesco and Wallenstein to Gustel, are based upon definite originals, while the *dramatis personæ* of " The Bride of Messina" are clearly not.   This is most apparent in Beatrice and Don Manuel ; and it is a severe task for art to give the latter any individuality of form.

The · artist has represented both the brothers as they stand in the presence of their mother—mute and defiant, with their wild retinues behind them.   Both are invested with the fire of youth, conjoined with princely dignity :

"*Donna Isabella* [*to Don Cæsar*].   In all the company
       . that hems thee in,
  Where is a nobler countenance than thy brother's ?

"[*To Don Manuel.*] Who, among these thou call'st
   thy friends,
Can to thy brother a moment be compared?
When you but think of his few years,
His equal will in vain be sought.".

Don Manuel's mode of thought confirms the mother's
portraiture of the two brothers:

" *Don Cæsar* [*without looking at Don Manuel*].
Thou art my elder; speak. Without dishonor
I yield to thee.
   " *Don Manuel.* One gracious word, and instant
My tongue is rival in the strife of love.
   " *Don Cæsar.* I am the guiltier, weaker.
   " *Don Manuel.* Oh! had I known thy spirit
      thus to peace
Inclined, what thousand griefs had never torn
A mother's heart!
   " *Don Cæsar.* Thou art too proud to meanness,
      I to falsehood.
   " *Don Manuel.* Say not so.
Who doubts thy noble heart, knows thee not well.
Thy words were prouder, if thy soul were mean.
   " *Don Cæsar.* We are one forever."

Love has made reconciliation easy for him; it has
extinguished the flame of hate. He is not only the
older but the more steadfast of the two brothers, as
we see in his words—

" Winged is happiness, and hard to bind;
Close locked, and set away, must it be guarded.

> Silence must be its constant sentinel,
> And quick it flies when tongues do prattle,
> And haste to lift the lid that hides it"—

yet he is not insured against the sudden attack of that overmastering passion to which his whole race is subject. We see this in the history of his love, where he has sudden recourse to force, and abducts the object of his passion before he knows whether it is absolutely necessary. He is always great, open-handed, pomp-loving; he even shows his fine taste in the selection of his bride's toilet! "Fair as a god, and manly as a hero," is the expression applied to him by her he loves; we see in him a proud and princely soul, and give him the whole measure of our admiration when misfortune has led him into that quarrel so long and protracted, that the traces left in his brother's soul are too deep to shut out envy and rage, when the least occasion for them appears—

> "The deeds accomplished are too marked
> To ever be forgiven or forgot"—

are the words of the chorus in view of the approach of Fate. They are of a piece with all that grandeur of diction which imparts so great a charm to the whole play, that even, aside from the treatment of the subject, the language itself has a powerful effect upon us. Everywhere we feel ourselves more exalted and blinded by the greatness of the poet's thoughts than by the fatal

spectacle which he places before our eyes. We feel
free, because we see ourselves lifted so high above all
that is low and mean. We do not understand the
workings of destiny, but we believe all the more
strongly in Schiller.

30

A.v.Ramberg del.   C.Gegen sculp

DON CÆSAR.

(*The Bride of Messina.*)

THE object of every work of art is to elevate us, and to give us a sense of freedom; that of tragedy in particular, to move us even to the foundations of our being. If "The Bride of Messina" attains, unquestionably, the first of these ends, we must, in candor, confess that it falls further short of the second than does any other of Schiller's plays. That this is the case must be chiefly ascribed to that false theory of his, adverted to on a foregoing page, according to which the poet detaches himself as much as possible from all local relations, and invests his characters with as few qualities as he can that connect them with us; he places them, so far as art allows him to do so, in an ideal world. If the fate of Mary Stuart, of Thekla, or of Louisa Miller, takes stronger hold of us, and they become dearer to us, it is from the number of individual traits which the poet has ascribed to them, and which he has denied to Isabella and to Beatrice; we know the epoch, the manners, all the environments of the former far better than we do those of the characters depicted in "The Bride of Messina."

We by no means give our love to what is perfect after its kind—in other words, the ideal—but to the incomplete, the imperfect, the individual. What is perfect puts us at a distance, only the individual is near us, and therefore allied to us, and intelligible.

We may carry this even further. As we take an interest only in what we understand, and cannot comprehend even the finest verses in a foreign tongue, so we love only that which has life. No one ever fell in love with the picture of a lady, notwithstanding the assertions of all the novel-writers. But it is only what has individuality that has life as well, and the secret suspicion that purely ideal figures have no capacity of life, never permits us to feel that interest in them which we have in those which have individuality. If the figures of Raphael, for example, excite our warmest interest, while those of the (perhaps) greater Michael Angelo seem far removed from us, and only fill us with a timid awe, there is no other reason for this than that the former wrought upon a basis of actual observation, while the latter embodied the mere creations of his own imagination.

We take an interest in Don Cæsar, so far as he displays to us individual characteristics; and, at all events, he is to us a more living personage than Don Manuel, because he possesses so much more individuality. The younger, he is, at the same time, the more ardent and

choleric of the two brothers—perhaps the nobler and
more magnanimous. He it is, at least, who takes the
first step toward a reconciliation; the more proud and
fiery, he is, at the same time, the one more easily won,
as he shows by his words—

> "Dost thou not think more meanly of the brother?"—

and—

> "Had I before known thee to be so just,
> Much now accomplished had been left undone."

Although passionate, like his whole race, he yet
hates intrigue with all the straightforwardness and
strength of a knightly soul; he punishes the traitor
who wants to assassinate Don Manuel for money. His
first thought, after gaining over his brother, is to give
him the whole love of his heart; and even more
vehement than his hate had been is the affection for
the newly-won friend—

> "More than I can tell
> Thy countenance delights me—firmly, I believe,
> We yet shall be the closest bound of friends"—

and he wishes to impart to his brother immediately the
new hope which has sprung up within his heart. The
brother, however, is little inclined to accept the confession:

> "Tell me thy heart! Keep to thyself thy secret."

Only into such a glowing nature as this, open to every
impression, can love enter like a flash of lightning, and
a single instant be decisive in its influence upon an entire

life ; and his previous want of acquaintance with love
must make him doubly susceptible.   Don Cæsar says
very ungallantly, when his mother bids him tell the
story of his love :

> "Thou know'st
> That, heedless ever of the giddy race,
> I looked on beauty's charms with cold disdain,
> Nor deemed of womankind there lived another
> Like thee—whom my idolatrous fancy decked
> With heavenly graces. . . .
>   Yet then the beams
> Of mighty love—so willed my guiding star—
> First lit my soul—but how it chanced, myself
> I ask in vain. . . .
>   In my heart,
> Though strange, yet with familiarities inwrought
> She seemed, and instant spoke the thought—'tis she,
> Or none that lives!"

The deep tenderness for his mother—a very fine
feature in both the brothers, finely invented by the
poet as an offset to their mutual hate—is particularly ·
beautiful in Don Cæsar ; and scarcely less attractive is
the zeal with which, despite his passion for Beatrice, he
goes to seek his sister, before he brings his bride to his
mother, and thinks only afterward of the need in which
his affianced is placed.

That he believes in Beatrice and her love, even
without hearing a word from her in confession of it, and
even ascribes her disquiet and alarm to the favor which
he thinks he enjoys with her, shows us afresh the stormy
excitement going on within him, and, as may readily be

conjectured in such characters, when he finds the one he loves in his brother's arms, all the old anger rises in him afresh, and, in the belief that he has been betrayed, drives him to the fatal deed.

All the more effectively does the thunderbolt of truth strike him—the man who, in whatever he does, means to do right—and he flies wildly to the bosom that bore him; even the old demon of jealousy regains its dominion over him, in spite of what has occurred, after he sees that his mother and sister have loved his brother better than himself. It is not his crime that forms his deepest grief, but his brother's possession of the heart of her he loves:

> ' Weep! I will blend my tears with thine—nay, more,
> I will avenge thy brother; but the lover—
> Weep not for him—thy passionate yearning tears
> My inmost heart. . . .
> I loved thee, as I ne'er had loved before,
> When thou wert strange; and that I bear the curse
> Of brother's blood, 'tis but because I loved thee
> With measureless transport; love was all my guilt."

It is the characteristic of great natures that they are not cast down and broken by adverse fates, but pierced and exalted by them; and Don Cæsar does not doubt for a moment that he is guilty of an offence, and that he must make an offering of himself to outraged justice, in order to do away with the curse which rests upon his house. This heroic character gives him the energy not only to resist his mother's entreaties—

> "Yes! in death are quenched
> The fires of rage, and Hatred owns, subdued,
> The mighty reconciler. Then to the tomb
> Stay not my passage; oh! forbid me not
> Thus with atoning sacrifice to quell
> The curse of Heaven. We pluck
> The arrow from the wound—but the torn heart
> Shall ne'er be healed. Let him who can, drag on
> A weary life of penance and of pain,
> To cleanse the spot of everlasting guilt;
> I would not live the victim of despair"—

but even, at last, to overcome steadfastly the petitions of his dearly-loved sister; the bright flame of love only gives him the power needed for the execution of what he purposes:

> "I will not rob thee, brother!
> The sacrifice is thine:—Hark! for the tomb,
> Mightier than mother's tears or sister's love,
> Thy voice resistless cries; my arms enfold
> A treasure, potent with celestial joys,
> To deck this earthly sphere, and make a lot
> Worthy the gods! but I shall live in bliss,
> While in the tomb thy sainted innocence
> Sleeps unavenged!"

Beatrice

BEATRICE.

THAT Schiller's poetic instinct always was a truer
guide to him than his theoretical reasoning, has already
been remarked in our comments on his portrait. "The
Bride of Messina" is perhaps the strongest proof of this,
as in this play the poet believed that he had reached
the highest point ever attained by him. Clinging as
closely as possible to the Greek form, he endeavored to
embody the Hellenic view of Fate—that which consigns
man to destruction without his own fault—a view which
is opposed to all our ideas of poetic and divine justice.
The result was, that he pleased the public best when he
followed his own genius most and his theory least;
whereas, with artists, it was just the reverse, and his
influence with them was unfortunate. It was Schiller's
brilliant example which led such men as Müllner, Wer-
ner, and others to write their "Dramas of Fate." Of
this fatalistic theory of predestination, which is exhibited
in "The Bride of Messina," there has been a dreadful
misuse made, and confusion has entered into all our

modern conceptions which have their foundation merely
in the free self-determination of man — a foundation
which appeared to be discernible on a superficial glance
at the unfolding of destiny in the princely family of
Messina.   Fatalism is indeed the chief element of the
Greek tragedy ; but, in Schiller's play, it has been by no
means retained in all its rigid logic ; as the destiny of
men is, in the main, the result of the collision of freedom
and necessity, so that of the hostile brothers, as well
as of their unhappy mother, springs largely from their
immoderation, and the boundless passionateness of their
characters ; external occasions merely give the stroke
that sets free what has been working within, and what
would sooner or later force its way.   Fate does nothing
more, primarily, than what the chorus hints at in its
words :

> " Yes, it has not well begun,
> Trust me, and it ends not well;
> No crooked paths to Virtue lead ;
> Ill fruit has ever sprung from evil seed !

The source of that misconception which has entirely
led Schiller's imitators astray is to be found, primarily,
in the character of Beatrice, whose happiness is wrecked
in the most fearful manner, in conformity to the biblical
saying, that the sins of the fathers are visited upon the
children unto the tenth generation.   This sin consists
not only in the abduction of Isabella—the curse-laden
source of all subsequent misfortune—but also in the heartlessness with which the father sacrifices his own child to

a dark superstition. Almost as great is the hardness of
her who began by deceiving her husband, and who, for
a long succession of years, has nothing to do with her
child, and even forgets her in three months after the
husband's death. Although this is the harbinger of
Fate, the poet has taken good care to show, in Beatrice,
despite the slightness of her individuality, the true
daughter of her mother, in making her guilty of a
double disobedience—in allowing herself to be taken
from the convent, and thus prevented by the blindness
of her passion from recognizing her mother; and in con-
travening the command of her mother and her lover that
she should not be present at her father's funeral. The
tragic element of the piece lies in the immoderate
severity of her punishment, the loss of her lover, brought
about by the inevitable workings of circumstances.

This tragical impression is heightened by the lofty
spirit which Schiller has given to Beatrice. Though he
has given her but a single scene in which to express her
inner nature, yet his delicate pencil-strokes enable us to
catch her character in some measure. The artist has
taken her in those scenes where, awaiting her lover, she
speaks out her consciousness of wrong-doing—

> "Forgot my childhood's ties,
> I listened to the lover's flattering tale—
> Listened and trusted! From the sacred dome
> Allured—betrayed—for sure some hell-born magic
> Enchained my frenzied sense—I fled with him,
> The invader of Religion's dread abodes!"—

and, in the most touching manner, she assigns the
cause—

> "And should I not surrender to the man
> Who, of all men, clung close to me alone?
> For all exposed was I to life's grave perils,
> And e'en a child, had fortune torn me
> (I dare not lift the dark, mysterious veil)
> From the embrace and bosom of my mother."

She then excuses herself, in thought, to her mother:

> "Forgive, thou lordly one, who bore me,
> That I, seizing with undue haste the tragic hours,
> Have brought my fate upon me with my own hands.
> Not freely have I chosen it; it has found me out."

The whole glow of Southern passion breaks out in
her when she says—

> "I know them not, and I shall never know them,
> Who call themselves the authors of my being,
> If they shall separate me from thee, my love.
> An everlasting riddle to myself I'll live;
> I know enough: I live for thee!"—

and, for this new offence, her destiny makes her its
victim immediately after Don Cæsar's appearance.

The hot blood of the race is seen also at the corpse
of Don Manuel, where Beatrice, awaking from her swoon,
accuses her mother for preserving her:

> "Oh, mother, mother! wherefore hast thou
> Saved me? Why did not you load me
> With the curse which followed me ere I breathed?"

> For my destruction, thine—yes, for us all
> Hast thou withheld from the˙ gods of the dead
> The prey they demand!"

Here we see that same singular mixture of Christian
and heathen ideas, which runs through the whole piece,
and often perplexes our whole moral feeling, despite the
wonderful splendor of the diction. This often has an
almost intoxicating effect upon the reader, and causes
us to cease to wonder that Schiller should think this the
greatest of his works. This mastership of art, indispensable as it is to a classic work, and prominent as it is in
this play, is not sufficient to put such a work as this in
the highest rank ; and, with respect to " The Bride of
Messina," we must confess that, in other pieces, Schiller
has come closer to the heart of the nation, and worked
with more effective power, or German culture and
German thought, despite the wondrous beauty of form
which he has given to the play now under consideration.

William Tell

WILLIAM TELL.

(*William Tell.*)

THE right of a free man, as well as of a whole people, not only to resist tyrannical oppression, but to battle even to the last, has never, perhaps, found so brilliant a defence as in Tell. Few as are the traces of the times in which he lived, upon the other works of Schiller, here they are unmistakable. Could the pressure of foreign dominion, which rested then so heavily upon Germany, have been without influence upon the thoughts developed in Tell? If, in Wallenstein, the hero and his command of men are unmistakably connected with the rising star of Napoleon, in Tell this relation to the circumstances of the time appears still more prominently. These noble words—

> "No, there are limits to the power of tyrants.
> When the oppressed has no more claims for right,
> And insupportable grows the load, he then
> With fearless confidence raises his hands to Heaven,
> And brings from thence his eternal rights.
> . . . .
> A last resort, when others fail,
> The sword remains"—

have become the watch-word of all those who have manly courage enough not to permit themselves and their rights to be trodden under foot; they contain the complete defence which mere force must appeal to, when all peaceful means are exhausted, and it must rely on itself alone; nay, they show that this is the only course that man can take.

Tell, in whom Switzerland's immortal love of liberty has found a worthy personification, is taken by the poet to be the centre of his drama, to show us the whole course over which a brave and religious people passes, step by step, in resisting the hand of tyranny, till at last it is driven to extreme measures. The picture is not a generalization, but a study of details.

Tell is a hero, but he is a peasant. He shows himself to be thoroughly a man of action, not of thought; like all heroes, he acts, not from reflection, but from a free nature; he is all of one piece. It is the physical courage, the Hercules nature, the nerves of steel united with a manly joy in self-sacrifice and danger, which stamp him as belonging to the circle of heroes. It is thus that he is introduced to us; it is thus that every one recognizes him, and unconditionally trusts his skill.

> "Far better men than I would not ape Tell,
> There does not live his fellow 'mong the mountains,

says Ruodi of him, after he has saved Baumgarten. This feeling of power, that marks him everywhere, makes him disinclined to take counsel, and join alliances; "the strong man is mightiest alone," he says, with entire correctness; "a true bowman helps himself," and, further on, trusting his instinct—

> " I was not born to ponder and select,
> But when your course of action is resolved,
> Then call on Tell, you shall not find him fail "—

for whoever thinks too much, does little.

Such consciousness of power, united with little inclination to reflect, is not conceivable without that joy in battle which Tell thus expresses—

> " I only feel the flush and joy of life,
> In starting some fresh quarry every day "—

and so he says to Gessler:

> " Were I a man of thought, I were not called the Tell."

Another sure mark of such a nature as his, is the readiness to answer every summons. Gessler is therefore perfectly correct in his judgment, when, in order to drive Tell to the last extremity, he turns him to scorn—

> " To hit the bull's eye in the target, that
> Can many another do as well as thou.
> But he, methinks, is master of his craft,
> Who can at all times on his skill rely,
> Nor lets his heart disturb nor eye nor hand.
> .   .   .   .
> Thy talent's universal, nothing daunts thee,

32

> Thou canst direct the rudder like the bow;
> Storms fright not thee when there's a life at stake.
> Now, savior, help thyself"—

and his own son is no less discerning when he says to
his father :

> " Quick, father, show them that thou art an archer.
> He doubts thy skill, he thinks to ruin us.
> Shoot, then, and hit, though but to spite the tyrant."

Equally shrewd in her judgment is his wife, when she
says of the deed :

> " Oh, ruthless heart of man ! Offend his pride,
> And reason in his breast forsakes her seat.
> In his blind wrath he'll stake upon a cast
> A child's existence and a mother's heart."

Deeply as she loves him, she feels this keenly. Cowards
fear before peril comes — brave men afterward ; Tell
sinks, convulsed, only after he has shot. This nature, so
little inclined to long speeches and soaring plans, still
holds one thought, to which it has been driven, all the
more fast. His determination to take Gessler's life
is all the more irrevocable, and even the boat-scene,
where a character more tamable would probably have
reckoned upon the favor of his opponent, does not
change his determination. The soliloquy, in which he
tries to justify his action, while lying in wait in the
empty street, has often been criticised, and yet, taken
apart from its rhetorical adornment, it contains merely
the motives that influence the soul of a brave, desper-

ate man, thoroughly aroused, fearing new disaster, and identifying himself personally with the whole contest. He feels that his adversary, having brought him by physical and moral compulsion to a place where he might have murdered his own son, has made a recourse to violence inevitable, for

"My children dear, my loved and faithful wife,
Must be protected, tyrant, from thy fury.
When last I drew my bow with trembling hand,
And thou, with murderous hand, a father forced
To level at his child, when, all in vain,
Writhing before thee, I implored thy mercy,
Then, in the agony of my soul, I vowed
A fearful oath, which met God's ear alone,
That when my bow next winged an arrow's flight,
Its aim should be thy heart!"

Tell is too thoroughly a hero to allow any thought of flight or concealment to stand in the way of the contest in which he means to avenge himself. He remains true to this as to a stern necessity, when he addresses the parricide :

"And dar'st thou thus confound
Ambition's bloody crime with the dread act
To which a father's direful need impelled him?
Hadst thou to shield thy children's darling heads,
To guard thy fireside's sanctuary? . . .
I have no part with thee, thou art a murderer.
I've shielded all that was most dear to me."

If we want to pass a correct judgment upon Tell's deed, we must remember the time in which it occurred, when

violence ruled, and force was met by force ; the personal
motives which are so prominent in his death, are seen,
in view of such circumstances, to be sufficient to explain
the act, and with righteous pride he says:

> " This hand
> Has shielded you, and set my country free.
> Freely I raise it in the face of Heaven."

A. Fleischmann sculp.

HEDWIG, TELL'S WIFE.

WITHOUT doubt, "Tell" is that one of Schiller's plays which contends with "Wallenstein" for the first place; although inferior in compactness to it, "Wallenstein" did not work so powerfully upon Schiller's contemporaries as this, his glorious swan-song. For this, it is in no slight measure indebted to the wondrous truthfulness of the local coloring which he has given to his picture, and which lends it a charm all the more peculiar and admirable, in the fact that, as is well known, Schiller never was in Switzerland, and knew neither the country nor the people from personal observation. But not only is the scenery depicted with unsurpassed fidelity, but the whole mode of thought and feeling of that pious, powerful, and self-reliant mountain-people is drawn with remarkable security of hand; and Schiller has succeeded in uniting this happy coloring with such splendor of diction, that many passages of the play please us like a strain from Homer. There strikes us,

indeed, the further similarity between these two great
poets, that the material of the "Tell," no less than that
of Homer's verses, lay ready at hand, capable of being
transformed into the most genuine of all poesy—that of
the people—and nothing remained but to give it the
artistic form. We may therefore put the "Tell" by the
side of the "Niebelungen" and "Faust," and regard it
as the third of our great national poems.

In this naturalness of coloring and bearing, the most
admirably drawn of all the characters is Hedwig, Tell's
wife, who claims our attention only in three short scenes,
and yet displays the whole mode of thought of a peasant-
woman. Loftier ideas—those directed to what is universal, those entertained by the more heroic, resolute,
and accomplished wife of Stauffacher—are remote from
her; her world is wholly in her own house, in her husband and children. For these she has a love which is
all the more touching that, as in so many other gentle,
womanly creations, it is most prompt to express itself
in a lasting fear about those for whom she lives; an
attempt to conceal her tenderness, whose inartificial and
naive expression deeply moves us when Tell says to her
that Nature never made him for a herdsman, and she,
thinking of his skill as a huntsman, breaks out:

> " Heedless the while of all your wife's alarms,
>   As she sits watching, through long hours, at home:
>   For my soul sinks with terror at the tales
>   The servants tell about your wild adventures.

Whene'er we part, my trembling heart forebodes
That you will ne'er come back to me again."

If, therefore, the artist has represented her in the
attitude of waiting for her husband, and thinking of
him, he has done so because thus the passivity and deep
feeling of her character are most distinctly expressed.
To the coarse and powerful form of the housewife,
undertaking all kinds of work, and active from morning
to night, he has had to unite a childlike and thoughtful
expression, gentleness, and a depth of feeling capable of
rising to the highest passion for her dear husband and
her loved children. She appears, perhaps, most lovely
when, in perpetual anxiety about him, she fails to understand his courageous daring in behalf of others who
are nothing to him; and yet there is a pride in him
that appears in every word as she reproaches him:

" Wherever danger is will you be placed;
On you, as ever, will the burden fall.
.   .   .   .
You took, ay, 'mid the thickest of the storm,
The men of Unterwald across the lake.
'Tis a marvel you escaped. Had you no thought
Of wife and children then? . . . .
To brave the lake, in all its wrath, was not
To put your trust in God—'twas tempting Him.
.   .   .   .
Yes, you've a kind and helping hand for all,
But be in straits, and who will lend you aid?"

Is that not said like a genuine housewife? To a
woman's nature, every thing that is general becomes

comprehensible only when it is invested with personality; it is love that makes her understand what self-
sacrifice is, and she sees it only in her own husband,
while those who are with him seem selfish and mean.
If fear does not comprehend the joy there is in danger,
it has all the sharper eyes for impending peril. With
what acumen she infers the wrath of the governor,
when Tell relates to her how Gessler had met him in
the mountains, and feared him :

> "He trembled, then, before you? Woe the while!
> You saw his weakness. That he'll ne'er forgive."

Entirely like a woman is it, also, that she allows herself
to criticise the husband whom she loves, and blame
his acts—

> "And he could wing an arrow at his child?
> . . . .
> Oh! if he had a father's heart, he would
> Have sooner perished by a thousand deaths. ·
> . . . .
> Were I to live for centuries, I still
> Should see my boy tied up, his father's mark,
> And still the shaft would quiver in my heart"—

and yet, as soon as any one else accuses her of a want
of feeling for him, she replies to Baumgarten and the
others with annihilating scorn :

> "Hast thou tears only for thy friend's distress?
> Say, where were you when he—my noble Tell—
> Was bound in chains? Where was your friendship then?
>   . . . . Did ever Tell
> Act thus to you?"

She now comes, for the first time, to a consciousness of her loss and grief. Passion makes her eloquent, and sharpens even her glance; and she, who had just found fault with him, now shows at once that she is perfectly aware what she and they all had lost in him :

> " Without him,
> What have you power to do ? While Tell was free,
> There still indeed was hope. Weak innocence
> Had still a friend, and the oppressed a stay.
> Tell saved you all—you cannot, all combined,
> Release him from his cruel prison-bonds."

But long, painful days must yet go by before the chains are loosened. The news of his deed fills her with shuddering fear, gradually to be converted into hope and joy, when she sees that it is the signal for the freeing of the whole land, and that he, whom she believed would be hunted down like a murderer, is now to return as the savior of his country. What thrilling emotions must pass through her breast! How beautifully is this return pictured, when the wife, carried away alike by grief and joy, announces their father to the children—

> "Boys, dearest boys, your father comes to-day!
> He lives, is free, and we and all are free !
> The country owes its liberty to him"—

and then, turning to Walter, who claims his share of glory, she says :

> "Yes, yes, thou art restored to me again.
> Twice have I given thee birth, twice suffered all

33

A mother's agonies for thee, my child.
But this is past. I have you both, boys, both,
And your dear father will be back to-day "—

and then, when she hears the step of her loved husband,
her voice fails her, her knees tremble ; in her agitation
she must cling to the door, in her rapture she can only
fall weeping into his arms!

Who, at the delineation of this beautiful and genuinely human scene, does not feel how much closer and
more blissful the bond that binds those who are happily
united in marriage, than that which connects mere
lovers ?

TELL'S SON.

(*William Tell.*)

WE have already spoken of the "Tell" as the immortal song of freedom, the fairest and most perfect bequest that the departing genius left to his nation. The immense influence which it has exerted can be best measured by the manner in which the nation received it, and entered into the possession of this heritage of its most eminent son. The reply may be found in the colossal struggle against foreign dominion, and in the shaking off of those shameful chains in which it had been bound through its leaders' fault or its own weakness. No other poet of the world has, probably, ever been able to glory in an influence upon his people so direct and so immense as Schiller. He shows us, as does no other, that it is the prerogative of powerful natures to form the mode of thought and even the character of their nation, and so to work effectively upon their history. What German is not filled with a just pride in the poet as well as in the people that bore him, when he looks at Germany as Schiller found it, and then regards

the year 1813 as the echo of the strains of our great
bard, the fairest monument that we could raise to him?

So all-pervading, in this drama, is the manly spirit of
freedom, of courage, of opposition to arbitrary power,
that it speaks out everywhere; even in the boy Walter
there breathes the reckless courage of a lion-like race.
The first instruction that we hear the father give his
boy—"a true bowman helps himself"—is certainly not
adapted to rear an effeminate child; and as little the
words—

> "But they shall learn it, wife, in all its points,
> Whoe'er would carve an independent way
> Through life, must learn to ward or plant a blow."

Courage is, in great measure, a result of education,
and Tell, as we see, knows how to increase it; but it
must also, to a great extent, like a taste for freedom and
independence, be born within a man. With Walter we
see both, for the first question which he puts, after the
enlargement of his geographical knowledge imparted by
his father, respecting the advantages of the lowlands
and their inhabitants, is:

> "Live they not free,
> As you do, on the land their fathers left them?"

And when that is answered in the negative, he does not
hesitate in his choice:

> "I should want breathing-room in such a land;
> I'd rather dwell beneath the avalanches."

Still more prompt is the youth in the thought of resistance; when his father is arrested, he does not content himself with complaining, but cries:

> "This way, you men;
> Good people, help, they're dragging him to prison!"

Defiance of danger is his strongest feeling; even when he sees every one around him trembling, he says—

> "Grandfather, do not kneel to that bad man,
> Say, where am I to stand? I do not fear"—

above every thing, he will not be bound:

> "Bind me?
> No, I will not be bound, I will be still,
> Still as a lamb, nor even draw my breath.
> But if you bind me I cannot be still,
> Then I shall writhe and struggle with my hands."

Just as little will he allow his eyes to be bound; the little heart is strong as steel, and it transports us to hear him say:

> "Quick, father, show them that thou art an archer.
> He doubts thy skill, he thinks to ruin us.
> Shoot, then, and hit, though but to spite the tyrant."

That he has not a trace of fear he shows us afterward, when alarm for his dear child completely unmans the father, and the boy calls out triumphantly:

> "Here is the apple, father. Well I knew
> You would not harm your boy."

It is natural that the artist should represent the lad at

this moment, and give us the little blond, radiant fellow, in whom good-nature and unbounded daring contend so amiably for precedence.

The never-ending struggles with Nature, in which the inhabitant of mountain-lands almost always finds himself, tend, very early in a man's life, to develop those qualities which qualify him to battle with other men: cool-blooded courage, presence of mind, and a proud, unbending reliance on his own courage in readiness at every moment of his life; whether he climbs the steep Alm as a shepherd, or descends as a hunter among the rocks and abysses of the mountain, amid the floods of the summer, or the thunders of the avalanche, or the roaring of winter storms, he is always in sight of danger. In these scenes there are developed not only a love of freedom and independence, but also that quickness of glance, and that keen intelligence which are common to all who dwell among mountains, and whose early traces in our Walter form so lively a picture. The little republican quickly becomes proudly conscious of his deed; and when his mother says — " The country owes its liberty to him," he instantly claims his share of Tell's glory :

> " And I, too, mother, bore my part in it.
> I shall be named with him. My father's shaft
> Went closely by my life, and yet I shook not."

Certainly the picture of the brave-hearted little fellow, as Schiller has drawn him, with his freshness and genuineness, is so natural a product of his rough and yet poetic home, that through the portraiture there breathes that same invigorating Alpine air which the poet has, in so masterly a manner, poured out over the whole drama. This marked local coloring that every thing in the "Tell" bears, which invests not only nature with splendor, but animates the men as well who live amid these colossal scenes, and which unites the two—man and nature—by so close and so powerful a bond that they cannot be separated one from another, is the chief charm of the piece; and in it Schiller displays a capacity of realistic delineation which far surpasses, in poetic worth, the idealizing pathos of earlier plays. The power by which he is often here enabled to sketch the whole scene by a few touches, and stimulate our fancy to fill it out, is so remarkable, that German literature has scarcely any thing to put by its side in respect of its pictures of nature, and few characters of greater freshness and amiability than that of our Walter.

Fr.Precht del.   A.Fleischmann sculp

Arnold of Melchthal.

ARNOLD VON MELCHTHAL.

(*William Tell.*)

IF in Tell the whole Swiss population of that epoch has its representative, and shows in him how manfully and ably, and under the stress of how great necessity, it pressed on to its goal, struggling for something which it recognized but did not completely understand, in Arnold we have the representative of newer times and later views : what appears unconscious and in its germ in all others of republican tendencies and burgher spirit, in him comes into complete and ready consciousness. He is the most striking representative of the future—of that great democratic movement which almost contemporaneously was passing through all German minds, and which culminated in most of the imperial cities with the downfall of patrician rule.

The hot-blooded youth is the quickest of all—ready with decision and action; he is the real soul of the attack—an Achilles in peasant's clothing. His prompt readiness breaks out everywhere, whether he shows us

how he has been carried away by his exasperation, and
paints to us, in relating the occasion of his flight, the
pitiable condition of the whole people beneath the yoke
of tyranny, and his own boiling anger—

> "Was I to brook the fellow's saucy words.
> That if the peasant must have bread to eat,
> Why, let him go and draw the plough himself? . . .
> On this I could contain myself no longer,
> And, overcome by passion, struck him down"—

and then, further on, speaks of his father—

> "I'm only sorry for my father's sake,
> To be away from him that needs so much
> My fostering care. The governor detests him,
> Because he hath, whene'er occasion served,
> Stood stoutly up for right and liberty"—

or when he replies to his old friend's warning, that the
tyrants are reaching out their hands to him:

> "They teach us Switzers what we ought to do."

At once, after hearing of his father's misfortune, he
breaks out:

> "Are we defenceless? Wherefore did we learn
> To bend the cross-bow, wield the battle-axe?
> What living creature but, in its despair,
> Finds for itself a weapon of defence?"

In like manner he flames up when Tell is captured

> "This is too bad. Shall we stand by and see them
> Drag him away before our very eyes?"

In one word, with him a quick deed follows a quick thought.

That he has not only a noble and grand nature, but is also a born party leader, is shown us in the manner in which his special misfortune leads him to measures which are general in their character. He does not find the means of contenting his revenge in any personal satisfaction, in taking the life of a single man as Tell does; he will have nothing less than the overthrow of the entire system of tyranny, and such a culmination he has in mind when he raises his hand to Heaven, and swears:

> " Alas! my old, blind father!
> Thou canst no more behold the day of freedom,
> But thou shalt hear it."

The artist has caught him at this instant, and represented him, not alone as the young hero, but as the peasant, for Melchthal is both of these. He, the representative of the plebeian element, is the counterpart to Rudenz, and he it is who first breaks with the old times. This he shows most clearly where Walter Fürst wishes to hear the counsels of those who have hitherto taken the lead—the noblemen of the land—to know what they will say respecting the compact that is to restore freedom to the land:

> " First let us learn what steps the noble lords
> Of Sillinen and Attinghaus propose."

He answers at once, and vehemently:

> "What need of nobles? Let us do the work
> Ourselves. Although we stood alone, methinks
> We should be able to maintain our rights."

Rudenz, who, likewise young, understands youth best, in sympathy with the democratic tendency, says correctly of it:

> "It fits their humor well to take their seats
> Amid the nobles on the herren-bank.
> They'll have the Cæsar for their lord, forsooth—
> That is to say, they'll have no lord at all."

The goal to which their views must certainly come is no other than that of complete independence, whereas the older men, at farthest, go to no greater lengths than Attinghausen, who defends half-way measures, and has in mind nothing higher than the idea of communal or provincial liberty. Melchthal is entirely opposed to these conservatives in his views about the future, although he is in entire concord with them respecting the measures to be immediately taken; therefore, when Stauffacher says—

> "And this alone should be the free man's duty,
> To guard the empire that keeps guard for him"—

Melchthal replies at once:

> "He's but a slave that would acknowledge more."

The trained politician, Attinghausen, discerns, at the outset, the tendency of which Melchthal is the youthful representative, and prophesies in sure presentiment:

"And have the peasantry dared such a deed
On their own charge, without the nobles' aid—
Relied so much on their own proper strength?
Nay, then, indeed, they want our help no more,
We may go down to death cheered by the thought
That after us the majesty of man
Will live, and be maintained by other hands. . . .
The old is crumbling down—the times are changing—
And from the ruins blooms a fairer life."

Most emphatic of all are Arnold's words, where he jealously glances from the leaders of the alliance to the nobility, and says to Rudenz—

"Take my hand,
A peasant's hand, and with it, noble sir,
The gage and the assurance of a man!
Without us, sir, what would the nobles be?
Our order is more ancient, too, than yours!"—

and so, when he relates what occurred at the taking of Sarnen Castle :

"Had he been nothing but our baron, then
We should have been most chary of our lives;
But he was our confederate, and Bertha
Honored the people."

Genuinely republican is he at the end, when he calls out, in tones of triumph :

"Thus, now, my friends, with light and merry hearts,
We stand upon the wreck of tyranny;
And gallantly have we fulfilled the oath
Which we at Rootli swore, confederates!

"*Walter Fürst.* The work is but begun. We
    must be firm.
For be assured, the king will make all speed
To avenge his viceroy's death, and reinstate
By force of arms the tyrant we've expelled.
   "*Melchthal.* Why, let him come with all his
     armaments!
The foe within has fled before our arms;
We'll give him welcome, warmly, from without!"—

and gives ready utterance to thought of unconditional
freedom.

Bertha of Bruneck.

BERTHA VON BRUNECK.

(*William Tell.*)

THE fresh, powerful character of the rich heiress, whose love-episode with Rudenz has been frequently attacked by critics, appears to us, nevertheless, not to be so superfluous as some have insisted that it is. If Rudenz appears entirely indispensable to the play, as the representative of that part of the nobility which, blended with the splendor of bearing rule, had succumbed to a foreign yoke, it is, unhappily, an only too true trait which has appeared at all times, especially with the Germans, and which, even in the time when Schiller wrote, was only too prominent in the Westphalian court and elsewhere. When Rudenz says to Attinghausen, " I am a stranger only in this house," and his uncle replies, skilfully portraying the entire worthlessness of the grounds which drive him to such a condition—

> ' Alas! thou art indeed! Alas! that home
> To thee has grown so strange! Oh, lily, lily,
> I scarce do know thee now, thus decked in silks,
> The peacock's feather flaunting in thy cap,

And purple mantle round thy shoulders flung.
Thou look'st upon the peasant with disdain,
And takest with a blush his honest greeting.
                    . . . . Thou alone
Art all unmoved amid the general grief.
Abandoning thy friends, thou tak'st thy stand
Beside thy country's foes, and, as in scorn
Of our distress, pursuest giddy joys,
Courting the smiles of princes all the while
Thy country bleeds beneath their cruel scourge"—

the relation of this picture to the sights which the poet
was observing is as little to be overlooked as that of
many other passages in "Tell."

Pitiful as are the grounds which Rudenz assigns for
his frivolous and faithless course—

"Yes, I conceal it not, it doth offend
My inmost soul to hear the stranger's gibes,
That taunt us with the name of peasant-nobles.
 .   .   .   .
'Tis vain for us to strive against the king,
The world pertains to him. Shall we, alone,
In mad, presumptuous obstinacy, strive
To break that mighty chain of lands which he
Hath drawn around us with his giant grasp?"—

they are, nevertheless, in the main, those which have
prevalence even in our own period ; and, at the time
of Napoleon, they were uttered with the greatest shame-
lessness by all dependants of the Rhine Confederation ;
and, for a long time, it helped little that the genuine
conservatives, the heroic characters in whom the German

nobility even then was by no means poor, replied, like Attinghausen, to the deserters:

> "No, if our blood must flow, let it be shed
> In our own cause. We purchase liberty
> More cheaply far than bondage. . . .
> Cling to the land, the dear land of thy sires,
> Grapple to that with thy whole heart and soul;
> Thy power is rooted deep and strongly here."

The youth, both of whose tendencies we see represented in Rudenz and Melchthal, must, in ushering in the new epoch, pass through their own special course of culture. Rudenz is brought to a happy issue by the sound and genuine nature of the lady who had knit her destinies to his, who shows the Swiss girl in every feature, although she does not belong particularly to the forest towns. Her bold heart beats with woman's loyalty to the home she loves; and what the reasons of the uncle cannot effect, her wrathful gentleness easily accomplishes, for no man, who has a spark of honor, can stand beshamed in the presence of her he loves. He can, however, be led astray by false premises and untrue systems, whereas woman always remains true to the great demands of nature, always returns readily to them. When, therefore, she confronts her misguided lover with the annihilating power of truth, and holds up to him the simple dilemma—

> "And dare you speak to me of love, of truth—
> You, that are faithless to your nearest ties? . . .

35

> Think you to find me in the traitors' ranks?
> Now, as I live, I'd rather give my hand
> To Gessler's self, all despot though he be,.
> Than to the Switzer who forgets his birth,
> And stoops to be the minion of a tyrant! . . .
> What dearer duty to a noble soul
> Than to protect weak, suffering innocence,
> And vindicate the rights of the oppressed? . . .
> But you whom Nature and your knightly vow
> Have given them as their natural protector,
> Yet who desert them, and abet their foes
> In forging shackles for your native land,
> You, you it is that deeply wound and grieve me"—

her logic is of that kind that a youthful spirit can scarcely resist. The straightforward, noble nature of the girl tears to pieces, as it were a spider's web, the trivial reasons which he gives to her, when he replies, as so many in the time of Napoleon did:

> "Is not my country's welfare all my wish?
> What seek I for her but to purchase peace
> 'Neath Austria's potent sceptre?"

Bertha is a genuine, fresh Alpine rose. She does not plume herself with the confession of the love she bears; she throws it boldly into the scale, in order to secure her lover to the righteous cause:

> "*Rudenz.* Bertha, you hate me, you despise me.
> "*Bertha.*   Nay,
> And if I did, 'twere better for my peace.
> But to see him despised and despicable,
> The man whom one might love!"

And that she really loves him is proved by the
impatience with which she bears the necessity of scorn-
ing him. But nothing works more powerfully upon us
than when any one speaks out his good opinion of our
character, and expresses a belief that we can do nothing
wrong. Seldom are we able to abstain from an attempt
to justify so good an opinion. When, therefore, Bertha
says, further—

> " No, no, the noble is not all extinct
> Within you; it but slumbers, I will rouse it "—

her victory is already won; for what lover could shun
an opportunity to show her he loves that he is noble ?

A woman, bold by nature, becomes fond of command,
and takes a part in the duties of man only when she sees
that he is failing in his duty, and becoming weak ; she
returns at once and all the more gladly to her sphere,
so soon as he returns to duty, and shows courage and
decision. Then she appears only as the loving wife,
careful for her husband's welfare. And so, if in the
first scene we have Bertha overmastering Rudenz with
her proud scorn, if she appears not only as the resolute,
rough German girl, but also as a member of the secret
opposition, she lets it all drop when her lover, returning
to his duty, fearlessly confronts Gessler with the words:

> " I have been dumb
> To all the oppressions I was doomed to see. . . .
> But to be silent longer were to be
> A traitor to my king and country both. . . .

> I madly thought
> That I should best advance the general weal,
> By adding sinews to the emperor's power.
> The scales have fallen from mine eyes."

She now thinks only of him, and seeks to hold him back ; the hero-maiden disappears, yielding before the loving woman, who, at last, finds her true home in the heart of the lover whom she herself has restored to his people.

GESSLER.

(*William Tell.*)

NOTHING is better adapted to awaken the sense
of justice, native to every man, than when they,
whose duty it is to administer justice, convert it into
its opposite, and turn the sway, in whose name right
and law are administered, from a blessing into a curse,
and shatter them. For all rule is given that justice
may be kept sacred. The instant when it denies this
first principle, it irrevocably brings into question its
own right to be. The most divine law ceases to be
so when an administrator of it demeans himself in
such a way as to satirize his own office.

But if a nature, arbitrary at the foundation, succeeds in gaining the power to administer law and justice, and takes advantage of their shelter in order to
promote its own whims and lusts, it grows, step by
step, more grasping and overbearing, and will inevi-
tably bring things into extremities on one side or
another.

The portrait of such an arbitrary and tyrannical

representative of supreme power is presented in Gessler
with such consummate skill as to make an impression
so deep that his name has become a proverb for despotism. ° True to his general method of making what
is human neither devilish nor divine, but simply subject
to counter-motives, the poet has painted this crafty and
malicious character in a manner which makes him at
least intelligible to us.

Deceiving himself and others, he seeks to justify his
native inclination to cruelty and hardness by political
motives—by that state-craft that has always been used
as a mantle to cover every thing base, and an appeal to
which allows him the pleasure of exercising a certain
measure of political activity, and of winning some
applause. He discovers, also, a means of giving his
cruelty a fair look ; it is the old doctrine of all tyrants,
constantly emerging into view, that the end sanctifies
the means, when Gessler says to Harras :

> " Say what you please. I am the emperor's servant,
> And my first care must be to do his pleasure.
> He did not send me here to fawn and cringe,
> And coax these boors into good-humor. No—
> Obedience he must have. We soon shall see
> If king or peasant is to lord it here."

And when Harras reminds him of the rights of the
people, in the true spirit of a despot he answers :

> " 'Twas not in sport that I set up the cap
> In Altdorf, or to try the people's hearts.

All this I knew before. I set it up
That they might learn to bend those stubborn necks
They carry far too proudly. And I placed,
What well I knew their eyes could never brook,
Full in the road which they perforce must pass,
That when their eye fell on it they might call
That lord to mind whom they too much forget."

Armgart thus reminds him of his duty :

" Justice, my lord—ay, justice ! Thou art judge,
The deputy of the emperor, of Heaven.
Then do thy duty : as thou hopest for justice
From Him who rules above, show it to us "—

and Gessler answers entirely in character :

" Hence ! Drive this daring rabble from my sight."

The governor cries out about impudence, as all do
who conceal their own worthlessness behind the majesty
of authority, and concludes by saying, as tyrants have
done in all ages :

"Too mild a ruler am I to this people ;
Their tongues are all too bold, nor have they yet
Been tamed to due submission as they shall be :
I must take order for the remedy.
I will subdue this stubborn mood of theirs,
And crush the soul of liberty within them."

This doctrine of unconditional obedience, of impudence
on the part of the oppressed, and of too great mildness
on the part of the oppressor, has it not always been
the dialectic of despotism ? We shall hardly err if we

conceive that the governor is a man who, long living
in a subordinate position, has succeeded in elevating
himself above the shoulders of other men, and revenges
himself threefold upon them for the treatment which he
has received. Our feelings are never wounded without
we seek to gain satisfaction, as we often see in the case
of subalterns, and even of soldiers ; nor can there be a
wound left in the spirit whose poison does not gradually
extend, and fill the system. This psychological development in the soul of the tyrant is all the more correctly
portrayed in the fact that, after he has been· driven
by a bad conscience to tremble before Tell—what no
man could forgive to him who caused his fear, least of
all a blood-loving tyrant — a way is opened to that
unheard-of cruelty with which he afterward treats
Tell, in order to compensate himself for his previous
fear.

Specially peculiar, and in the genuine spirit of the
·Middle Ages, is the touch of humor in Gessler ; he feels
himself comfortably situated, and inclined to jest in his
rôle of tyrant—a sure proof that he is acting out his
nature, and not something which has been superinduced.
The goal which he places before Tell corresponds more
or less to the wild and rough, yet adventurous character
of the time ; it indicates the scorn with which the aristocrat was accustomed to look down upon the plebeian.
The despotic instinct is also well defined, where Gessler
disputes the ancient privilege of the people to carry arms :

"The proud right which the poor hind assumes
     Offends the country's highest lord;
   No one should arm himself but he that rules."

The tyrant's arrogance is naturally increased by the antagonism of a few fearless natures, who generally fall the first victims, while the masses only gradually become familiar with ideas of opposition, and, remembering the sacrifice of their brethren, are at length aroused to a combat for life or death.   Thus a despotic temper, apparently strengthened at first by a temporary gratification, must necessarily either destroy a ruler, or reduce the conquered people to an apathetic serfdom, where every vestige of independence is destroyed.   The poet, in his description of the simple and undeveloped life of a shepherd race, expresses this universal and impressive truth, that, among an oppressed people, nothing healthy can flourish—no inspiration of the human mind in poetry or art can succeed, nor can any advancement be looked for even in the rudest material science ; and that, therefore, the first duty .of him who will not renounce the desire of human progress, is resistance to despotism.

36

A. v. Ramberg del.   G. Jaquemat sculp.

TURANDOT.

THE proud Turandot is a twin-sister of our northern Brunhilde, with this difference, that the former makes the competition of her suitors intellectual, while the latter commits it to physical strength. They are personifications of that maiden pride which revolts against the thought of submission. Both these women have strong natures, full of the consciousness of their own power, and rebel especially against the idea of becoming the possession of any man, because neither of them had as yet met with a lover who had impressed her with his superiority.

In Turandot we see how it was impossible that her weak father, or any of his courtiers, could instil into her mind the idea of the subjection of her sex, since the poet was careful to represent those surrounding her as either contemptible or ridiculous. If we could be malicious, we might infer, from this disposition for contest, that both women, in their inmost hearts, nursed the wish to be conquered.

It is also evident that the crowd of crazy lovers,
greedy for her dowry, could not increase the esteem of
Turandot for the male sex. She will have no master
who is not worthy to rule her, and whose merit she is
not forced to acknowledge, in his possession of dis-
tinguished-intellect and courage. Hence come the proposed enigmas to her suitors, as well as the results with
which she threatens them. It is but reasonable that he
who aspires to so great a prize should be worthy of it;
that he should possess sufficient penetration to discover
her thoughts, however obscured by words; that he
should have presence of mind not to lose, even for a
moment, complete control of himself, in view of the
terrors of death, as well as of the bewildering power of
beauty, and while, at the same time, the strongest of
passions is raging in his own bosom. If we find this
cruel, Truffaldin replies with all authority:

> "There's no command that princes take their necks
> To Pekin—no one calls them hither. . . .
>   We strike
> No head from him who brings it with him.
> Already has he lost who stakes it here!
>   . . . . Every one can woo:
> Nothing is easier than to journey
> As a suitor. He lives at no expense,
> Pampers himself, and makes the generous house
> Of his desired relative his home.
> How many a younger son or needy squire—
> Whose carpet-bag gives room for all his goods—
> Subsists upon his love's rejections!

Sometime this place was like a hostelry
Where came proud princes and adventurers,
Who wooed the emperor's wealthy daughter.
E'en the meanest thinks himself quite worthy
To embrace the maiden's peerless beauty.
Thus, comrade, you may see how honest
Is the princess with her eager suitors :
Before marriage she dispenses riddles—
Afterward, indeed, it would be worse ;
For he is lost who cannot solve the words
His wife proposes during marriage ! . . .

    " *Brigella.* Well, I care not—let them be enigmas,
If thus she has the whim to show her wit.
But must it be that amorous princes
Lose their heads because they cannot tell
Her hidden meaning ? That is barbarous ;
Reason nor honor can have part therein.
When did you ever hear that loving men
Must die for what is hard to understand ?

    " *Truffaldin.* And, blockhead, how could she avoid
        the fools—
Who think presumption is their wisdom—
If they perchance had nothing else to risk
But once to be disgraced in the divan ?
No one would shrink to venture on the ice,
If all the danger were a harmless fall.
Who fears th' amusing puzzle ? 'Tis a play
Of words enlisting thought and making mirth ;
And those who, for the witty princess' sake,
And her great treasure, might have stayed at home,
Would come for the solution of her thoughts ;
For few think less of their own mental skill
Than of the wealth and beauty of a spouse ! "

Even if the faculty that solves all the problems

makes the suitor worthy of a throne, it does not of
Turandot's heart, since an intellectual and courageous,
but, at the same time, emotionless and merely ambitious
man, might obtain her.   It is this error in her calcula-
tion that fills her with apprehension when Kalaf appears,
and so easily masters her wisdom.   The uncertainty,
whether love—which is the only return for love—will
be reciprocated, drives her to desperation.

Moreover, a profound anxiety occupies Turandot's
heart, because she hears within herself a voice speaking for Kalaf—she is sensible of the power which this
stranger exerts over her, and, on his first entrance,
she says:

> . . . . ' No one yet entered
> The divan who e'er could win my love.
> But this man knows the art."

Proud and strong natures always rebel against that
which would conquer them : it is the reaction of an
intact, healthy temperament against the sweet poison
of love.   Even in the common affairs of life, any one has
the right to set his own price on himself, and the only
question is, whether he will find a purchaser ; but it
proves that one has a just estimate of himself if he is
readily appreciated.   Turandot's pride has forced her to
demand the highest stake—the venture of her own life—
and she is right, because no one ought to unite another
life with his own, if he is not ready to give his own for
it.   Every man seeking wedlock should be willing to do

this. There is consequently no cruelty in the desire of the princess, however quaint and difficult the manner in which the fable is represented.

Though Kalaf has shown that by his endowments he is worthy, yet much is wanting to enable Turandot to be certain of his love; she therefore confesses hers only after she has made him pass through trial—when she, on her side, has conquered him by the solution of a problem— since by this it was in her power to give herself freely to him, as being the most deserving, after having assured herself of his love by his noble demeanor in temptation.

The artist has represented to us the charming sphinx in the act of drawing aside her veil, after she has propounded the third enigma to Kalaf; hoping to confuse him by her overwhelming beauty, and thus bear away a double triumph, of which, however, she is not sure, though she will not acknowledge her fear. We cannot dislike her in this mental struggle, since we know how great her humiliation must be, if, after all that has happened, she finds herself conquered. The more precious the metal the more intense must be the fire that is to melt it.

...have a soul like him... ...of feeling which originated in... ...it understands them better than their author... ...ce shows us the scarf of Coz? faithfully... constructed as "Turandot" much better, they... himself by means of Brighella and Truffaldino's rough... ancho-Panza-like wisdom he validates in their ludicrous... dialogue, the principal idea...

One of the characteristics of our poet is the almost... ful absence of naiveté. He is always conscious, and... has but little pleasure in the play with its finish or... *laissez aller.* The genial capriciousness of the muse does... t suit him. He places it involuntarily in... undation by the concise grandeur of his...

KALAF.

WORKS of art are organizations like man himself, and have a soul like him—that is, a transference of the intellect or feeling which originated them; and yet another often understands them better than their author. Thus Schiller shows us the soul of Gozzi's fable, which he reconstructed as "Turandot," much better than Gozzi himself; by means of Brigella's and Truffaldin's prosaic Sancho-Panza-like wisdom, he exhibits, in their burlesque dialogue, the principal idea.

One of the characteristics of our poet is the almost total absence of naïveté. He is always conscious, and so he has but little pleasure in the play, with its fantastic *laissez aller*. The genial capriciousness of the fable does not suit him. He places it involuntarily on too real a foundation, by the concise grandeur of his language, and the distinctness of his sketches. He fills up his figures with a truthfulness and consequence, by the side of which the mere story reminds us of theatrical tinsel in the presence of really precious vestments. The creation of the

87

Italian was ingenuous, and it was sufficient for him to
relate a curious tale, from love of the wonderful, not of
the deeper meaning therein contained. With Schiller
the reverse is the case : as a philosopher it is a necessity
with him to discover the secret import of facts, especially
of those the most strange ; to follow the traces of a
flighty play or a voluptuous fancy, and reveal from what
idea or sentiment it arose ; to bring out this its soul into
full light, and let it grow in the sunshine of his intellect.
At least thus he treated Gozzi's child's fable ; he understood it aright, and brought it to maturity and meaning.

The poet indicates his greater intelligence by the
manner in which he introduces the two principal characters—Turandot and Kalaf—giving a motive for every
action, especially ascribing to the prince those qualities
that alone can attach a high - spirited and imperial
woman.

Kalaf has seen life in all its phases, and passed
through the severest trials with a strong and sound
mind. Though cast from the summit of happiness into
the deepest misery, notwithstanding his manly resistance,
yet adversity could not weaken his heart, nor change his
regal mode of thinking. He always met misfortune with
courage, and humiliation with pride, permitting them to
gain no ascendency over him. He might be precipitated
from a throne, but his noble nature could not be sullied,
while, at the same time, he became more experienced
and resolute. Thus only could he be dangerous to one

like Turandot—a woman seeking not a love-sick boy, but
a friendly and true man.

With great wisdom, the poet gives him another
qualification that must endear him to a lady jealous of
admiration, and who considers it the greatest triumph to
conquer one hitherto unmoved by temptation : he has
never loved, but in fact despises the female sex.   He
abhors the strategy of Turandot, which appears a mere
caprice, until love opens his eyes :

> " And does such idiot live who ventures thus
> His life for wealth or heartless beauty ! . . . .
> How could holy Nature make a monster
> Armed against all human love and mercy ?
> Down to the dark abyss of Tartarus
> With this Turandot and those who, like her,
> See naught to love but what is in themselves ! "

Kalaf laughs at the possibility of falling in love with
the princess, when Barak wishes to prevent him from
contemplating her portrait :

> " You are not wise.   But if *you* feel thus weak,
> I am not so.   No woman's beauty e'er
> Hath pleased these eyes, even for a moment,
> Much less subdued my heart.   And surely what
> No living, smiling charms could e'er effect
> Fears not the colors of the artist's brush.
> Vain is your care !   My mind, good Barak,
> Has other occupation than love's folly."

There are fields of sentiment, as well as of thought,
that remain hidden until some accident suddenly reveals

them to our mental vision, affording us an insight into an unimagined world, which cannot fail to surprise ānd interest us.

Thus it is with Kalaf, in reference to love and women. He despises them because he has never known the heavenly influence of a union of beauty and intellect, having always noticed in his own experience that the one did not imply the coexistence óf the other in the same person. But if he had not abhorred Turandot, her portrait would not have made such an enchanting impression on him. He is the more affected just because he judges her harshly—because he has no idea of the happiness resulting from the possession of a noble woman's heart.

As yet, however, egotism is mingled with this sentiment, for he also considers the dowry of the bride when he resolves to risk all to gain her·:

> "Barak! betray me not.—Now or never!
> This is the trying hour of my fortune.
> And why prolong a despicable life?
> The die being cast, I gain a woman
> Fairest of earth's daughters, and an empire—
> Or lose what then becomes a hated life."

As with Turandot, so with Kalaf—love must soften and purify him before a true union can take place. This process of the gradual elevation of the passion to magnanimity and devotion, the poet has represented with the inimitable hand of a master, for Gozzi was too sensual to have had a conjecture of what is essential to genuine love.

The artist has painted Kalaf while solving the first problem, having as yet a full consciousness of his superior intellect, so that an ironic smile wreathes his lips; the adventure pleases him, and he betrays a secret sense of success. The rapid changes in life so frequent at Oriental courts induce an enjoyment in what is unusual and hazardous; it was therefore absolutely necessary to introduce this element in the person of the prince.

DEMETRIUS.

ONE of the most distinguishing traits of Schiller's genius is political insight—an acute penetration into state affairs—a profound understanding of the life of nations in general, and of each in particular. In this respect, he manifests in his writings, considering the simplicity and seclusion of his life, an almost incomprehensible gift of anticipation. It seems, indeed, incredible that his little journeys from Stuttgart to Weimar could have given him such power of delineation in reference to characters differing so much in race and education. We can, in a small degree, account for this by the fact that, between the years 1792 and 1805, representatives of nearly all the nations of Europe passed through that district. The unceasing struggle of his day is certainly reflected much more in Schiller's muse than is generally conceded, for the noise of battle may be heard not only in " Wallenstein," but in " Tell," and the " Maid of Orleans." We see in them all the armed movements of the spirit of his time.

But nowhere do we find that rare political and national insight more brilliantly at work than in the fragment " Demetrius." The description of the Diet, which opens the piece, is unsurpassed. We fancy we see this Polish *régime* before our very eyes—that restless aristocratic republic, with its unending intrigues and frivolities. We recognize everywhere · the national instability, faithlessness, and . moral corruption, but sometimes also a chivalrous knighthood, and a . superabundance of intellect, while, at the same time, we are reminded of the universal lack of practical sense and tenacity, so that that unhappy country appears as a badly-counselled and spendthrift youth. How the Poles could easily conquer, but not retain—how they felt the heroism of physical contest, but were callous to civic virtues, and loved the war - horse, but despised the plough—all this is represented very skilfully in "Demetrius." No history could so well describe the anarchy of the "Polish Diet" as those few scenes which the poet devotes to its sessions, and which give the impression that the nation, notwithstanding some noble qualities, was incapable of a high civilization.

The filling up of the several parts is as excellent as the general sketch. The influence of the women is especially noticed, beautiful, intellectual, and patriotic, as they were, but also ambitious and cunning, and who find their representative in Marina. The power of the clergy over the popular will is also inimitably portrayed.

Equally well, so far as the work extends, are the Russians contrasted with the Poles. Both are Slavonian races, distinguished by semi-barbarous manners, an easily-excited imagination, and a pleasure in intrigue. The Russians, however, have the advantage of greater attachment to their dynasty, and a more willing submission to authority; they are less independent, but more faithful and honest.

With this background appear the two figures of Marfa and Demetrius—the former terrifying us with her thirst for revenge. German poetry has given us nothing more impressive than the scene where she thinks she has the means of retaliation in her hands:

> " Oh, I can at last my heart unburden,
> And speak of vengeful but restrainéd hate!
>   . . . . Who was it that exiled me,
> Opening a tomb for one who was not dead,
> But breathing in the bloom of youth's fresh strength
> With all its pure and loving sympathies?
> Who tore away my son, forever dear,
> And bargained with assassins for his life?—
> Maternal sorrow has no words to tell
> Of the long watches in the starry night,
> When yearning I looked up to righteous Heaven,
> And seemed to doubt its justice by my tears!
> The tardy hour of vengeance is at hand—
> Already are the mighty in my power. . . .
> It is my son!—I cannot doubt it—
> It is he! and with him moves an army
> To free his mother, and avenge her wrongs!
> The sweet wind, kissing my wearied brow,

38

Tells me of trumpets and the martial tread
Of the deliverer. Come from your steppes
In the north, and from the southern forest-shade,
My friends of distant climes and varied tongues !
Come, countless as the angry ocean-waves,
And gather to the standards of your king !
. . . . Oh, sun, bear on your radiant wings
My hope ; and thou, the unimprisoned air,
That quickly makest distant voyages,
Convey to him my passionate longing !—
I have nothing now but these my prayers,
Which, wingéd from my loving inmost heart,
I send to Heaven for thee, my son ! ”

Demetrius engages our sympathy by his honesty and
firm belief in his right—a sympathy increased by the
intelligence and subtlety with which he finds means to
gain adherents. He is represented at the moment when
he affirms to the Polish Diet his claims to the throne of
the Czars, showing as a proof the cross hung around his
neck at his baptism.

Demetrius indicates everywhere the Slavonic characteristics in the highest degree : eloquence, quick perception, inherent sagacity, and good-nature, as well as
excitability, and attacks of unbridled anger, in one of
which he kills a rival ; and, in another, the man who had
substituted him in place of the true prince. The poet
was obliged to reveal as much as possible this dexterous,
panther-like trait, as well as the love for barbarous pomp,
distinguishing the Slavons.

If this fragment of a tragedy gives unfulfilled promise

of a masterpiece, it can only heighten our sorrow that death called Schiller so early from his labor, when he had just become perfect in art, and would, doubtless, have given to the world many other evidences of transcendent genius.

THE PRINCE.

(*The Ghost-Seer.*)

THE moral of Schiller's celebrated novelette " The Ghost-Seer " is, that, if we give but the little finger to the tempter, he will soon take the whole man. It gives us the history of the conversion to Catholicism of a German Protestant prince, representing to us his character and fate — a chef-d'œuvre of psychological development.

Bred at a North German court, the third prince of the blood, he had little hope of ascending the throne. His education had not been properly attended to, for he had received no high connected culture ; what he had resulted only from superficial knowledge, the necessary languages, and very desultory reading, as is the case with many of his equals in rank. Such reading, resorted to in ennui, and merely intended to pass the time, had greatly excited his fancy, and, aided by the unpleasant circumstances in which a younger prince always finds himself, rendered him reserved, absent-minded, and meditative. As the best refuge, he entered the army at an early age,

and was in several campaigns. The service gave outward
dignity to his character, while experience strengthened
his natural peculiarities. Thus passed his youth, but a
divided existence between the duties of the camp and a
species of day-dreaming, as well as an inherent and
acquired timidity, had prevented him from associating
with women, so that at the age of thirty-five, and notwithstanding his fine exterior, he was a novice in respect
to ladies' society. Add to these antecedents the limited
means of a younger prince, whose position, being entirely
dependent on the throne, is always a miserable one, and
it is easily explained why a passionate and confiding
character should be inclined to gravity, or even to melan-
choly. Incompleteness of education, as well as the list-
lessness induced by a want of useful occupation, aids
greatly, in such a case, to incline the mind to the contemplation of the novel and mysterious. It is much
easier to see wonders, and believe miracles, than to
study the laws of life and Nature, especially when one is
of an indolent and obstinate temperament. In such circumstances the mind—when conscious of the presence of
evil-disposed spies—entertains a kind of aversion to what
is real, and a profound desire to catch a glimpse of the
spiritual—that is, to be deceived. Thus our prince follows, without much thought, the allurements of the
Armenian and the Sicilian. It is at the incantation-
scene that the artist represents him, making prominent
his courage and calmness in supposed danger. The

sound common-sense which he betrays, when afterward judging of these deceptions, is quite relative, as from the beginning he shows too much readiness to believe in the supernatural.

The need of deep religious impressions is here manifest. The prince has become acquainted with Protestantism from its grim fanatic side, which sees in works of art only the enticements of the Evil One, and in life itself nothing but a preparation for death. No wonder that this form of faith did not attract him.

The first illusions in reference to modern miracles, as well as pride in his power of discernment to expose them, lead him naturally into unbelief, for both the falsehoods of superstition and the falsehoods of infidelity are well known to have control alternately in the human soul. Skepticism advanced so much the nearer to him, as in the last century it was extensively associated with aristocratic privileges, which gave to it a sort of character. Religion in the prince's youth had appeared to him always in a most repulsive form—as a wearying system of espionage. But while he gradually frees himself from the bigotry of Protestantism by his own exertion, and inclines to the bigotry of unbelief, he cannot help glorifying himself in his conquest; he strengthens his independence, and diminishes the former distrust of his own judgment. When one begins to admire himself, he soon expects admiration from others; he needs and seeks flatterers, and, if a prince, he is sure

to find them. At first he listens gladly, and finally believes them.

This gradual change in a naturally modest and retiring character is very well described, as also the fact that,
when such change has proceeded to a certain extent,
momentous consequences are often the result.

His usual reserve has forsaken the prince; he first
delights in being brilliant, as a woman, merely by personal appearance—without any assistance from considera-
tions of rank—but he soon uses them to promote the
respect he covets. This produces larger pecuniary ex-
penditure, ending in disorder and disgust. A man of
princely position becomes thereby ill-humored, and hence
appears a stronger inclination to amusement. He wishes
to flee from the uncomfortable reproaches of his own
mind, and rushes into still greater difficulties. Instead
of acknowledging the blame, he ascribes it to others, and
feels the necessity of silencing, if he can, the voice of
conscience. He is in that state of excitement when
love, in its most seductive form, easily conquers a heart
hitherto proof against temptation.

It is therefore clear that the object of the prince's
violent passion—the Grecian maid—must have great
influence over a nature such as his. We have sufficient
motive for his conversion to Catholicism in the death of
this beloved person, considering the respect with which
he regards her memory; in his irretrievable financial
embarrassment, united with estrangement from his former

religious principles ; in the longing for some new
and mystic system, offering him consolation for the
sudden loss of his beloved and redemption from earthly
troubles, while, at the same time, the bonds uniting him
to his home are apparently and without cause broken
asunder.

39

A.v.Bamberg del.   C.Gonzenbach sculp.

THE GRECIAN MAID.

(*The Ghost-Seer.*)

It is well known that "The Ghost-Seer" was originally intended to appear in two parts, though we have only received the first. The second was probably designed to make us better acquainted with the fair unknown, who only appears toward the close, in a kind of episode, which at best is but fragmentary, and calculated to arouse our curiosity. As the heroine, she does not further the action of the plot, the prince being already far gone toward Catholicism without her personal presence or her prayers.

He meets the supposed Grecian maid first at church, and describes her appearance in so vivid a manner that the painter introduces her as she was then seen, "half-kneeling, half-prostrate, near the altar," dressed in black moire-antique, "that, closely fitting her arms and waist, flowed around her like the rich folds of a Spanish robe; her long blond hair, in two broad plaits, had fallen, of its own weight, from beneath her veil, and lay in disorder on her shoulders; one hand rested on the crucifix, ·

and, gently inclining, she supported herself with the other." This picture suits better a German than a Grecian girl, and it finally appears that she is a German beauty, who, under the glowing sky of Italy, awakens in the prince a passion altogether unconscious of the charms of any fair Venetian.

The manner in which the handsome incognita is announced : first, as the friend or beloved of the Armenian, who plays the principal intriguer's rôle ; then, as if she also inflamed the heart of the Marquis Civitella ; afterward painted as a Madonna, purposely put up for sale ; and, finally, as the fair devotee or penitent in the chapel,—all this makes us suspect her of being a confederate of the Armenian, the cardinal, and the marquis, in their difficult undertaking of converting the prince. Nevertheless, Schiller remorselessly lets her die, just to give more emphasis to the part she played. The prince's companion writes : "During the ten days of her illness he never slept. I was at the *post-mortem* examination. There were traces of poison. She is to be buried to-day." So she was no deceiver, but really loved the prince, and was the friend, perhaps even the daughter, of the Armenian, since we hear of her mother only, a German lady of rank, and of the persecutions of a certain noble who forced her to take refuge in Venice.

The solution of this riddle Schiller would probably have given in his second part of the " Ghost-Seer," which he still owes us because he thought it would not have repaid the trouble of writing. But, in truth, it seems as if the author had had no determined plan, and that his object was the conversion of the prince, leaving the rest to accident or caprice—to some inspiration that might aid him in the details, and which gave him already, in the Grecian maid, a lovely German, of whom we would gladly know more. As it is, her death does not agree with her appearance on the stage, especially as we are informed, from the correspondence of Schiller with Lotta, that the poet intended her merely as a bait to attract the Protestant to Catholicism.

Without troubling ourselves with the solution of questions that belong to the tale as it exists, or following the traces leading to the source whence Schiller borrowed his materials, let us glance again at the unfinished novel, as it is the only work not having dramatic pretensions of which our illustrations treat. And yet the special genius of the author asserts itself more in this than in any similar contemporary production. Every thing here develops itself dramatically, as well as in his two histories, where the events which pass without comment before our eyes are the most interesting. The unfolding of character, step by step, out of the circumstances surrounding it, and its power, in turn, over them, marking every paragraph with progress, is so much in the manner of Schiller's writings, that he does not forget it anywhere.

The interest never flags. We are always in suspense.

There are none of those numerous episodes, or imitation
of that broad epic style characterizing Goethe's novels.
We are kept close to the principal object; all inferior
scenes are in connection with it, and receive no more
attention than to make them illustrate the chief person-
ages.   And these never speak as in Goethe, merely to
utter profound or beautiful remarks, applicable anywhere, as if the author prided himself on the depth of
his intellect, or the complacency of his wisdom.   Schiller's characters speak only to advance the action, and
reveal themselves.   In "The Ghost-Seer" the prince is
a dramatic success, quite unlike Goethe's workmanship,
whose figures appear finished from the first, and resist
every change which might naturally arise from the
incidents and progress of the story.   Here, on the contrary, we clearly see the secret modifications of character, and the realization of a purpose which we could
not have surmised.

As Schiller marvellously illustrates the inner life of
man, so also does he know how to employ outward
Nature, and the temporary surroundings of his heroes,
never failing to bring them to his aid in securing the
desired effect.   In reading "Tell" the glorious Alps
seem to be part of the play—they prepare the heart
for the emotions awaiting it.   He seemed, in fact, to
have a very intimate acquaintance with scenery that his
eyes never beheld, as in "The Ghost-Seer."   Here we
have the noisy throng, and there the mystic and silent

life natural to Venice and the adjacent islands. His portraitures, in a word, are all perfect, and, notwithstanding his inclination to philosophy, he had not yet reached the inference, that, if words are intended to conceal thought, colors are therefore meant to misrepresent the reality.

THE END.